THE LAST YEARS OF
YORKSHIRE STEAM

PETER TUFFREY

GREAT N-ORTHERN

ACKNOWLEDGEMENTS

I would like to thank the following people for their help:

Paul Bolton; Ben Brooksbank; Matthew Brown, Yorkshire Wolds Railway; David Burrill; Nigel Callaghan; W.A. Camwell; Nick Catford, Disused Stations Website; Paul Chancellor; Neil Cholmondeley; David Clay; Barry Cox; Nicholas Cox; Ron Fisher; Peter Jary; Frank Jones; David Joy; John Law; Patrick O'Brien; Kerry Parker; Hugh Parkin; Keith Platt; John Platt; Derek Porter; Richard Postill; Bill Reed; A.M. Ross; T.E. Rownthwaite; Peter Sedge; Andrew Stopford; Andrew Warnes; Bill Wright; Sue Warnes; Anthony Watson, A1 Steam Locomotive Trust; David Webdale of Lost Railways of West Yorkshire Website; Bill Wright; Alan Young; Syd Young.

Special thanks are due to my son Tristram for his help and encouragement throughout the project.

PHOTOGRAPHS

Every effort has been made to gain permission to use the photographs in this book. If you feel you have not been contacted please let me know: petertuffrey@rocketmail.com.

INFORMATION

I have taken reasonable steps to verify the accuracy of the information in this book but it may contain errors or omissions. Any information that may be of assistance to rectify any problems will be gratefully received. Please contact me by email: petertuffrey@rocketmail.com – or in writing: Peter Tuffrey, 8 Wrightson Avenue, Warmsworth, Doncaster, South Yorkshire, DN4 9QL.

Great Northern Books
PO Box 213, Ilkley, LS29 9WS
www.greatnorthernbooks.co.uk

© Peter Tuffrey 2016

ISBN: 978-0-9933447-4-9

Design and layout: David Burrill

CIP Data
A catalogue for this book is available from the British Library

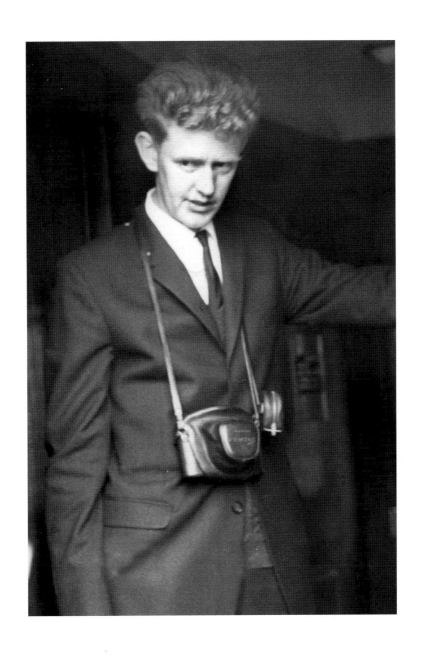

THIS BOOK IS DEDICATED TO
GEOFF WARNES (1935-2015)

INTRODUCTION
BY DAVID JOY

No county in England surely offered quite the same variety in the last years of steam as did Yorkshire. There was a wonderful array of locomotives in settings ranging from cathedral cities to grimy mill towns and from glorious countryside to thriving coastal resorts. This book is a celebration of their stamping ground, with locations arranged alphabetically to highlight the amazing contrasts that were on offer from the years following nationalisation in 1948 until steam on British Railways officially ended twenty years later.

Yorkshire stood out from the crowd in once being served by seven separate railway companies. The Lancashire & Yorkshire, London & North Western and the Midland became part of the LMS, while the Great Northern, Great Central, North Eastern and the Hull & Barnsley were absorbed into the LNER, so the rivalry never quite ended. In terms of wasteful competition it was still in evidence when steam drifted into its steady decline in the late 1950s.

Dominating the county's railways were the two Anglo-Scottish main lines. The East Coast route from King's Cross was largely a level playing field, entering Yorkshire via the great railway centre of Doncaster and then curving into the magnificent station at York before heading like an arrow across the plains towards Darlington. Completely different was the Midland route from St Pancras, emerging from a tunnel at Dore to descend to the 'steel city' of Sheffield prior to threading its way through the coalfield to Leeds. Here most trains reversed, running past countless woollen mills in the Aire Valley and finally facing the challenging climb to leave Yorkshire on the heights of the legendary Settle-Carlisle line.

Only slightly lower down the ladder in terms of spectacle were two cross-country routes linking the other side of the Pennines with 'God's Own County'. The main line from Manchester to Leeds pierced the watershed in the depths of Standedge before reaching the architectural glories of Huddersfield station. More indirect was the earlier line down the Calder Valley past mill chimneys galore with its steeply graded offshoot to Halifax and Bradford. Just as important

were the routes from Doncaster to Hull and from York to Scarborough, where the terminus long retained such a splendid array of semaphore signals. There were many others, apart from a whole plethora of branch lines heading in all sorts of directions for reasons often unclear.

The photographers who recorded steam on such a diverse variety of railways deserve our deepest gratitude. They certainly had the essential quality of patience. It is easy to forget that intensity of passenger traffic has grown enormously in recent years and even on the trunk routes there was in steam days nothing like the same frequency of trains. Apart from Saturdays, York was famous for its 'dead hour' between 3pm and 4pm when not a single train moved. In the summer months there was at least the consolation of earlier seeing 'The Elizabethan', with the likelihood that an immaculate Haymarket A4 – not normally seen south of Newcastle – would be on the up or down non-stop service linking London and Edinburgh.

Most lines depicted in these pages have since changed out of all recognition, often for the better with electrification of key routes and also the odd surprise such as the Ilkley branch. Equally, many have gone altogether. A sizeable section of the East Coast Main Line was diverted as part of an abortive bid to extend deep-level coal mining, leaving Selby served by solely the cross-country route from Leeds to Hull. Especially sad is closure of the link between Northallerton and Harrogate via Ripon, once carrying through services between Newcastle and Liverpool. Recalled in a series of poignant pictures is the heyday of Whitby, reached by lines from York, Scarborough and two routes from Middlesbrough. The ravages of the Beeching era left just the questionable choice of a single-track railway down the Esk Valley route as a withered shadow of former times.

Even on lines that have survived, it is often only too obvious that the glory has departed. A smartly turned-out Compound, waiting to depart from Bradford Forster Square with an impressive rake of corridor carriages, is a reminder of the days when the 'Residential Express' took woolmen back to their seaside villas at Morecambe in just a shade over 90 minutes. Try making that journey today, with a change at Skipton and then a long ride on a diesel unit often more noted for its rattle than its comfort.

It has to be admitted that these photographs also depict railways that either should never have been built in the first place or had no hope once motor buses and lorries whittled away the scant remaining traffic. The extravagant scale of a station such as Great Horton merely reflects the misplaced optimism of lines attempting to serve Queensbury, which were among the most heavily engineered in Yorkshire and can never have made a penny. Or take Little Weighton, with its nearest settlement no more than a tiny village on the Hull & Barnsley Railway built as a competitive route that was largely needless.

It was all hopelessly uneconomic, as witnessed at Chapeltown by stations only a few hundred yards apart on rival Great Central and Midland lines. Where one of these companies went in South Yorkshire the other, like Mary's little lamb, was also sure to go. At the other end of the scale was Edlington Halt, a mere bed of sleepers at track level on the Dearne Valley Railway. It simply succumbed, although others met a more lingering fate. Grassington & Threshfield lost its passenger services as early as 1930 but thirty years later was still fully signalled with its own station-master and porter-cum-signalman. The same staffing level is shown at remote Sledmere & Fimber on the Yorkshire Wolds where there was certainly time to spare in handling just the occasional pick-up goods.

Pictures are a clear remainder that freight workings were all too often far from a payload, be it the shortest of fish trains at Bempton or just one milk tanker being brought through Stainforth from the Express Dairy at distant Appleby. No matter how few wagons there would still be a driver, fireman and guard to pay. Gradually it all had to change and so too did much of the wonderful railway atmosphere of the 1950s and '60s. Stations handling everything from livestock to household furniture would soon become a distant memory, as would scenes such as Conisbrough station platform bustling with baskets of live pigeons.

Locations mean little without locomotives and again

Yorkshire was noted for an almost bewildering variety. Here were to be found everything from the Pacifics of the East Coast Main Line and the Royal Scots and Jubilees of the Midland route down to heavy freight motive power and humble shunting engines. Photographers were certainly prepared to seek out the seldom seen, as instanced by the S1 class of 0-8-4 tanks normally confined to Wath marshalling yard. Considerably more glamorous were the B17 4-6-0s, named after stately homes or football teams, which generally ventured no further north than Sheffield Victoria on a through service from Harwich.

Elsewhere, there was plenty on offer at the many lines serving the then flourishing coalfield with the great incentive that steam continued well after its 1968 demise on British Railways. Few scenes could be more evocative than Denaby Main Colliery washery with a saddle tank perched on high against a backdrop of pit winding gear and chimneys belching smoke. Blackness was everywhere but colour was still to be found, as shown by the pair of tank engines at Wheeldale Colliery in contrasting green and red liveries.

It was the locomotive sheds that epitomised the steam age, and images of Huddersfield, Manningham, Mirfield and Scarborough are just some of many that reflect the glory and the grime. The sheer hard labour is captured in a sad scene at Leeds Holbeck with a locomotive in filthy condition being prepared for service alongside diesel power that in a matter of months was to oust steam at this depot.

Conditions got worse as the end drew nigh, but at least enthusiasts aplenty were ready with their cameras to record the last few years. It became a race against time in capturing key moments – a quest made all the more urgent by the woeful lack of ex-LNER locomotives destined for preservation. Survivors were ever more neglected, and it is hard to tell that Jubilees *Ulster* and *Hogue*, respectively seen at Doncaster and Sheffield, had ever sported a smart green livery.

The final and lingering death throes involved the cutting up of once proud locomotives for scrap at such locations as Doncaster Works and Draper's Yard in Hull. They are almost too distressing to contemplate but can scarcely be avoided in a book that sets out to portray the last years of Yorkshire steam through to the very end. May such an age never be forgotten.

Opposite top ALNE STATION

Alne station was opened on March 31, 1841 by the Great North of England Railway. During 1891 a bay platform was added for the Easingwold branch line. The station closed to passengers on May 5, 1958 and completely, 10 August 1964. Passing through during July 1959 is Class A4 4-6-2 locomotive no. 60012 *Commonwealth of Australia* with 'The Elizabethan' train. Before withdrawal in August 1964, no. 60012 was allocated to Ferryhill shed Aberdeen. Photograph courtesy of *Yorkshire Post Newspapers*.

Bottom right ARMTHORPE MARKHAM MAIN COLLIERY

Robinson Class O4 2-8-0 locomotive no. 63670 manoeuvres coal wagons at Armthorpe's Markham Main colliery sidings. The line serving the colliery ran, south to Low Ellers junction and north to Kirk Sandall junction. Coal was reached at Markham Main in 1924; closure came in February 1996. Photograph taken on March 23, 1963 by Geoff Warnes.

Below ACTON HALL COLLIERY

Airedale, the locomotive depicted at Acton Hall colliery, was built in 1923 by Hunslet. The locomotive spent time at other pits in the Airedale Collieries group before arrival at Acton Hall in January 1963. On December 22 1975, *Airedale* went to Embsay for preservation. Acton Hall colliery, dating from 1877, closed in July 1985. Photograph by Bill Reed.

ALNE STATION

Class A4 4-6-2 locomotive 60013 *Dominion of New Zealand* hurries through Alne station with 'The Elizabethan' express, a daily non-stop train between London and Edinburgh. The service was introduced in celebration of the new Queen Elizabeth era. Departure from both ends – King's Cross and Edinburgh – was at 9.30 am for a teatime arrival after a journey of 393 miles. After entering traffic in June 1937, the locomotive was withdrawn from King's Cross shed in April 1963. Photograph courtesy of *Yorkshire Post Newspapers*.

Above ANSTON

Stanier Class 8F 2-8-0 locomotive no. 48673 heads a mineral train along an embankment at Anston on May 9, 1964. At this time the engine was allocated to Kirkby-in-Ashfield. Withdrawal came after 23 years and five months in service during October 1967. Photograph by Geoff Warnes.

Below ARDSLEY SHED

At Ardsley shed on February 21, 1960 is Class J52 0-6-0ST locomotive no. 68869 alongside Class V2 2-6-2 locomotive no. 60861. Ardsley was the last allocation of both engines. A shed at Ardsley had existed from 1860 but the one here from 1892. Closure came in October 1965 followed by clearance of the site. Photograph by Geoff Warnes.

Opposite top ARDSLEY

Taken from a bridge just west of Ardsley station the view depicts Gresley-designed Class J50 0-6-0T locomotive no. 68941 (erected at Doncaster Works March 1926) leaving the Bradford line and heading an 'Up' local goods train. Ardsley station was opened on October 5, 1857 and closed on November 2, 1964. The locomotive only survived until the end of the year being withdrawn from Bradford Bowling Junction shed on December 31, 1961. Photographed by Ben Brooksbank on April 22, 1961.

Opposite bottom ASKRIGG STATION

The *Yorkshire Post* of April 19, 1954 said an energetic campaign had failed to retain the passenger service on the Wensleydale branch railway line from Northallerton to Hawes. Askrigg station is pictured during the last day of operation on April 26, 1954. Opened by the North Eastern Railway Company, the station was situated on the stretch of line between Leyburn and Hawes. The section between Leyburn and Askrigg opened on February 1, 1877; and to Hawes on June 1, 1878.

Below ARKSEY

Situated on the East Coast Main Line, Arksey station, partially seen on the right, opened on June 6, 1848, and closed August 5, 1952. Robinson Class O4 2-8-0 locomotive no. 63653 was in service between April 1918 and April 1966. Photograph taken on August 7, 1965 by Geoff Warnes.

Above ASKERN COLLIERY

Askern colliery flourished between 1911 and 1985. Rapid loading of British Railways coal trains brought to an end the use of standard gauge locomotives at the pit in 1980. Robert Stephenson & Hawthorns Ltd built 0-6-0ST *Norman* in 1943, works no. 7086. The engine was noted at Yorkshire Main colliery, Edlington from at least January 1947 and transferred from there in April 1970 before being written off in June 1976. From Askern the locomotive went to Titanic Salvage Co. Ltd, Ellastone, Stafford in January 1977, then moved to Kent & East Sussex Railway, Tenterden, Kent. It is currently located at the Embsay & Bolton Abbey Railway. Photograph taken on May 27, 1975 by Geoff Warnes.

Opposite top ARTHINGTON

Edward Thompson's rebuilt *Cock o' the North* 4-6-2 locomotive, no. 60501, is heading southwards, through Arthington, on the Harrogate-Leeds line constructed by the Leeds & Thirsk Railway. Opening in 1848, the line extended north from Leeds to Harrogate Brunswick station (until 1862), via Leeds Wortley Junction, Headingley, Horsforth, Arthington, Weeton and Pannal. Arthington Junction station was opened, to serve the Otley branch and the Leeds-Harrogate line, on February 1, 1865. Until that time, an earlier station, Pool (renamed Arthington 1852), had existed further north from July 10, 1849. Arthington Junction station closed on March 22 1965 and the site has been cleared.

Opposite below ARTHINGTON

Travelling along the Harrogate-Leeds line, A3 Class 4-6-2 locomotive no. 60085 *Manna* approaches Arthington Junction station from the north having just crossed over Pool Bridge. The line to the left leads to Otley and was completed by the North Eastern Railway Company on February 1, 1865. Closure to passengers came on March 20, 1965 and freight 5 July 1965; Arthington North Box is to the right. Built at Doncaster Works, *Manna* entered service on February 22, 1930 and was withdrawn from Gateshead, October 12, 1964. The photograph, courtesy of *Yorkshire Post Newspapers*, was taken during February 1958; the Harrogate-Leeds line is still extant.

BARNSLEY SHED

Barnsley shed was situated on the east side of the town's Exchange station. Comprising two through roads, the shed at its northern end included a turntable. The building was given a gable-style roof around 1956 but closed on January 4, 1960 and the site cleared. On the immediate right is Robinson-designed Class O4 2-8-0 locomotive no. 63697, entering service during June 1918. The engine was allocated to Barnsley on January 8, 1950 and remained there until a move to Langwith Junction occurred on November 29, 1959. Adjacent is Gresley-designed Class J39 0-6-0 locomotive no. 64902, which entered service in August 1936 and was allocated to Barnsley between November 1956 and January 1960. Geoff Warnes took the picture on August 16, 1959.

Above BARNSLEY SHED

Built at Vulcan Foundry in 1904, Class J11 0-6-0 locomotive no. 64376 was at Barnsley shed from March 1957 until withdrawal in November 1959. Standing adjacent is Class J11 0-6-0 locomotive no. 64302 noted at Barnsley shed from July 1953 until withdrawal in September 1958. Photograph by Bill Reed.

Below BARNSLEY SHED

Class C14 4-4-2T locomotive was built by Beyer Peacock Ltd in 1907. Allocated to Barnsley in July 1957, the engine was withdrawn during December 1959. Photograph by Bill Reed.

Above BAWTRY

Situated approx. 147 miles from King's Cross and nine miles from Doncaster, Bawtry was also about one mile from Scrooby Water Troughs. Level at the water troughs, the line rises at a gradient of 1:198 approaching Bawtry before it falls at a gradient of 1:198 between Bawtry and Rossington. The line becomes level again between Rossington and Doncaster. Class V2 2-6-2 locomotive no. 60981 hurries under a bridge along the Great North Road near Bawtry c. 1958. Emerging from Darlington Works in April 1944, the locomotive was allocated to York, moving to Darlington in July 1953 then returned to York two months later, from where it was withdrawn in April 1963. During a lifetime of fractionally under 19 years, the engine travelled 664,973 miles. Scrapping occurred at Darlington Works a month after withdrawal. Photograph by Bill Reed.

Opposite top BAWTRY

Class A4 4-6-2 locomotive no. 60029 *Woodcock* races in open countryside at Bawtry c. 1958. Built at Doncaster Works, the engine entered service in July 1937 and was the second A4 to carry the *Woodcock* name. No. 4489 (later 60010) entering service in May 1937 was the original holder until becoming *Dominion of Canada* from June 1937. The second *Woodcock*'s first allocation was to Gateshead then Doncaster, King's Cross, Gateshead, King's Cross and New England being withdrawn from there in October 1963. In January the following year, scrapping was undertaken at Doncaster. Photograph by Bill Reed.

Opposite below BAWTRY

Class A1 4-6-2 locomotive no. 60122 *Curlew* is also depicted at Bawtry c. 1958. Entering traffic from Doncaster Works in December 1948, the engine was named in July 1950. First allocated to King's Cross, no. 60122 would move to Gateshead, Copley Hill, Grantham, King's Cross again and Doncaster before withdrawal from the latter shed in December 1962. Unlike a number of other A1s, *Curlew* worked few goods trains and its last logged trip was the 'Harrogate Sunday Pullman' on November 11, 1962. Cutting up was carried out at Doncaster in January 1963.

Above **BEIGHTON STATION**

Facing south, and pictured on February 3, 1950, is Beighton's third station, opened by the Manchester, Sheffield & Lincolnshire Railway on November 1, 1893. Comprising two brick buildings, each one had extensive canopies stretching to near the platform edge. The surrounding area was prone to flooding, often affecting the station, as can be witnessed here. Curiously, in the early 1950s, the track-bed and platforms were raised to help alleviate the problem, yet the station was closed on November 1, 1954 and the site subsequently cleared. Robinson Class O4 2-8-0 locomotive no. 3583 (later no. 63583) is displaying a single lamp denoting a train of empty mineral wagons. Built by the North British Locomotive Company, Glasgow (NBLC), the engine entered service in November 1912 and was withdrawn on June 30, 1959 from Sheffield Darnall. Photograph courtesy of *Sheffield Newspapers*.

Opposite top **BEIGHTON**

Road developments in the Beighton area as well as the removal of Brookhouse colliery on the right make the area virtually unrecognisable today. The view is facing north along the old North Midland – Derby, Rotherham, Leeds – main line opened in 1840. Working a coal train, Stanier 8F 2-8-0 locomotive no. 48161 entered service from Crewe Works during February 1943, being withdrawn in September 1967. The last allocation was 9F Heaton Mersey. Photograph taken by Ben Brooksbank on July 13, 1963.

Opposite below **BEMPTON STATION**

Travelling north past Bempton station and hauling a short train is Gresley Class K3 2-6-0 locomotive, no. 61875. The station is situated on the 13 mile stretch of the former York & North Midland's line between Filey and Bridlington, which opened on October 20, 1847. Designed by G.T. Andrews, the station is thought to have opened in May the following year and is still operational. Built at Doncaster Works and entering service during July 1929, no. 61875 was allocated to Hull Dairycoates before withdrawal on December 12, 1962. Photograph taken by Ben Brooksbank on April 18, 1961.

BELL BUSK

In a view looking over to Otterburn Moor and Kirkby Fell, Stanier Class 8F 2-8-0 locomotive no. 48157 heads south east towards Bell Busk station with a freight train on the ex-Midland main line. Note the engine is fitted with a snow-plough. Out of a total number of 666 8Fs, no. 48157 was one of 130 built at Crewe Works and entered service in December 1942, surviving until May 1967. The entire 8F Class was in service between June 1935 and August 4, 1968. Photograph taken on April 21, 1961 by Ben Brooksbank.

Above BIRKENSHAW & TONG STATION

Class J50 0-6-0T engine no. 68941 hauls a short freight train through Birkenshaw & Tong station on April 22, 1961. The train is travelling west on the Laisterdyke to Ardsley line opened in its entirety by the Leeds, Bradford & Halifax Junction Railway on October 10, 1857. Birkenshaw & Tong station opened on August 20, 1856 and closed to passengers October 5, 1953, goods September 7, 1964. Entering service from Doncaster Works during March 1926, no. 68941 was withdrawn on December 13, 1962, the last allocation being Ardsley. Photograph by Ben Brooksbank.

Below BOLTON ABBEY STATION

On the old Midland Skipton – Ilkley line (opened in 1888), ex-War Department 2-8-0 locomotive no. 90451 approaches Bolton Abbey station from the south east. The line closed to passengers on March 22, 1965. The Bolton Abbey – Embsay section of the line was opened by the Embsay & Bolton Steam Railway Trust from May 1, 1998. Photograph taken on April 21 1961 by Ben Brooksbank.

Above BRADFORD LOW MOOR MPD

The original shed at Low Moor was built by the Lancashire & Yorkshire Railway in 1866 but replaced just over 20 years later with a 12 track dead-ended building. Amongst the facilities were a coal stage, water tank and turntable. This shed was rebuilt in 1948 but closed on October 2, 1967. On the left is Stanier-designed Jubilee Class 4-6-0 locomotive no. 45565 *Victoria*. Built by the NBLC, the locomotive entered service on August 18, 1934 with allocations to Holbeck, Low Moor, Wakefield and finally Low Moor again before withdrawal in January 1967.

Opposite top BRADFORD EXCHANGE STATION

Exchange station was opened on May 9, 1850 by the Lancashire & Yorkshire Railway. The building was rebuilt in 1880 with ten bay platforms and two arched roofs. Closure came on January 14, 1973. A new smaller station was opened approx. 50 yards south on part of the old Bridge Street Goods site. By 1977, a bus station had been built alongside and on May 16, 1983 the entire complex was titled Bradford Interchange. Looking towards Bridge Street, Fairburn Class 4P 2-6-4T locomotive no. 42287 was photographed by Geoff Warnes on February 11 1967. Built at Derby Works the engine entered service in October 1947, the last allocation being Wakefield prior to withdrawal in July 1967.

Opposite below BRADFORD

With a good head of steam, Fairburn Class 4P 2-6-4T locomotive no. 42073 was photographed at Bradford by Geoff Warnes on January 8, 1967. At this point, the engine was allocated to Low Moor and moved to Normanton in July 1967. Withdrawal from there occurred in October of the latter year.

Above BRIDLINGTON

Built at Vulcan Foundry, War Department 'Austerity' 2-8-0 locomotive no. 79264 entered service in February, 1945 and became BR 90704 from August 1951. Withdrawal occurred in June 1967 and the engine was scrapped in December 1967 at Draper's Yard, Hull. The locomotive is depicted crossing to Bridlington station which was opened on October 7, 1846 by the York & North Midland Railway Company. The station was designed by G.T. Andrews and included an overall roof. Alterations were carried out in 1873-74, 1892-93, 1912, 1961, and 1983. Photograph taken on October 26, 1964 by Richard Postill.

Opposite top BRADFORD FORSTER SQUARE STATION

Bradford Market Street station was opened on July 1, 1846 and rebuilt in 1890, becoming known as Bradford Forster Square station on June 2, 1924. The last trains ran from there on Saturday June 9, 1990, before a new redeveloped station was opened adjacent two days later. Derby Works-built Compound Class 4-4-0 locomotive no. 41112 prepares to depart with an express passenger service for Morecambe in April 1957. The engine was in service between November 1925 and November 1957, withdrawal occurring from Lancaster Green Ayre. Photograph by T. E. Rownthwaite.

Opposite bottom BRIGHOUSE

Viewed from the Huddersfield Road over-bridge facing west, Stanier Class 4MT 2-6-4 tank locomotive no. 42622 passes through Brighouse station. An earlier station, built by the L&Y, began services on October 5, 1840, but was replaced by a larger one, depicted here, to the west of the original site and it opened on May 1 1893. This survived until January 5, 1970 and was replaced by another station opened on the same site on May 28, 2000. Built by Derby Works, no. 42622 entered service on July 13, 1938. The last allocation was 55A Holbeck before withdrawal in February 1967. Photograph taken by Ben Brooksbank on April 22, 1961.

Above **BRIDLINGTON**

The first Bridlington shed, with two tracks, existed between 1875-1893. Another shed opened to the west of the original building in 1893, and comprised three tracks, a slated gable roof, turntable and water tank. The building was closed by British Railways on December 1, 1958 but survived until 1986. Thompson Class B1 4-6-0 locomotive no. 61087 is depicted at Bridlington shed on August 16, 1963. Built at NBLC, the locomotive entered traffic on October 16, 1946 and was allocated to Sheffield Darnall. Withdrawal was from Doncaster on December 12, 1965. Photograph taken on August 16, 1963 by Richard Postill.

Opposite **BRIDLINGTON**

With Bridlington Town Hall tower in the background, Class B1 4-6-0 locomotive no, 61306 is pictured manoeuvring near the town's goods yard. In 1956 the station accommodated Medforth & Co's siding and the North Eastern Gas Board siding. An eight ton crane was also available. Built by the NBLC, no. 61306 was in service from April 5, 1948 to September 30, 1967. The engine was sold, in working condition, on February 1, 1968 for preservation. Photograph taken on April 21, 1965 by Richard Postill.

Above BRIDLINGTON

WD 'Austerity' 2-8-0 locomotive no 90704 is entering Bridlington station from the goods yard on October 26, 1964. Facilities once available at the station were provided for goods traffic; passenger, parcels and miscellaneous traffic; furniture vans etc; live stock; carriages and motorcars by passenger or parcels train. Photograph by Richard Postill.

Below CADEBY

Cadeby colliery existed between 1893 -1986. Costing the Denaby & Cadeby Colliery Company £1650, Peckett Class X 0-6-0ST locomotive *Firsby* was built in 1900 and delivered in July of that year. The engine was rebuilt in 1926 by Hudswell Clarke & Co. and scrapped on site during July 1973. The photograph, which shows the locomotive near a platelayer's cabin, was taken in April 1959 by Frank Jones.

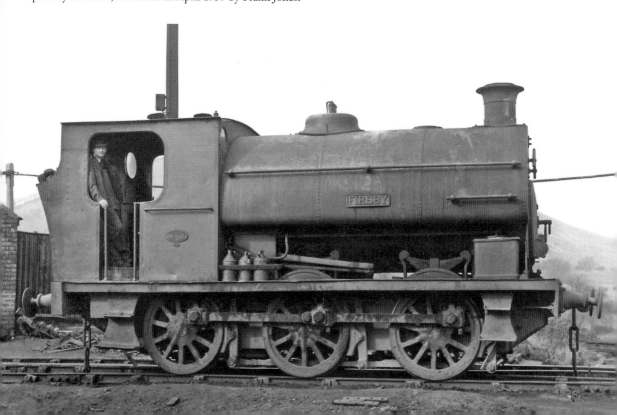

Above CADEBY

Andrew Barclay 0-6-0ST locomotive no. 35 is in the loco shed yard at Cadeby colliery. Built in 1923, the engine was employed at Tinsley Park colliery, Kilnhurst colliery and Cortonwood colliery before arrival at Cadeby in 1962. During April 1973 no. 35 was scrapped at Cadeby. Photograph taken in 1970 by John Law.

Below CALVERLEY & RODLEY STATION

Fowler Class 4P 2-6-4T no. 42394 is hauling the Leeds to Bradford section of the St Pancras to Bradford express through Calverley & Rodley station on June 26, 1964. Photograph by Ben Brooksbank.

Above CANKLOW

Canklow shed was built south of Masborough station by the Midland Railway in 1900, and featured a triple gable roof, a ramped coal stage and a water tank. BR closed the shed on October 11, 1965 and it survived as a factory before demolition during the 1980s. A housing estate now covers the site. Class 2F 0-6-0 locomotive no. 58238 is located at the south end of Canklow shed, with the area to the right extending over the River Rother and to West Bawtry Road in the distance. Designed by W. Johnson, no. 58238 was built at Derby Works, and stayed in service from January 1885 until November 1957. Photograph taken on March 15, 1953 by Geoff Warnes.

Opposite top CASTLEFORD STATION

The original Castleford station was opened by the York & North Midland Railway on July 1, 1840 but was resited further west by the NER in 1871. Between 1953 and 1969 the station was known as Castleford Central. Darlington Works-built Class G5 0-4-4T locomotive no. 67319 was in service from December 1900 to December 1957 being withdrawn from Malton. Photograph from the David Joy collection.

Opposite below CHAPELTOWN CENTRAL STATION

Chapeltown station was opened on September 4, 1854 and renamed Chapeltown & Thorncliffe June 1895, Chapeltown Central June 18, 1951 and closed December 7, 1953. Class C13 4-4-2T locomotive no. 67409 was withdrawn from Barnsley shed in December 1956 after over 53 years in service. The C13 locomotives were noted for working on both suburban and branch line duties. Photograph by W.A. Camwell.

Above CHAPELTOWN SOUTH STATION

Chapeltown South station was only a quarter of a mile away from Chapeltown Central. It was opened as Chapeltown by the Midland Railway on July 1, 1897 and was known as Chapeltown South between June 18, 1951 to February 20, 1969. The station was resited on August 2, 1982. Class 5 2-4-2T locomotive no. 50646 is fronting a push-and-pull service from Barnsley Court House station during November 1955. Photograph from the David Joy collection.

Opposite top CONISBROUGH STATION

On May 3, 1955, an unidentified Class B1 4-6-0 locomotive is approaching Conisbrough station from the west with the 08.40 (08.00 from Sheffield Victoria) to Doncaster. At one time the station had sidings for Kilner's Glassworks and the NCB's Cadeby Main. There were also facilities for live stock, horse boxes and prize cattle vans. Note the men with pigeon baskets on the left. Pigeon traffic ceased on British Railways on July 1, 1976. Photograph by Doug Brown.

Opposite below CONISBROUGH, RIVER DON BRIDGE

With Cadeby colliery in the background, Jubilee Class 4-6-0 locomotive no. 45593 *Kolhapur* heads west with an excursion over the bridge crossing the River Don at Conisbrough. Completed at NBLC in December 1934, *Kolhapur* worked all over the LMS system from St. Pancras to Derby, Nottingham and Manchester, from Leeds to Carlisle and from London to Birmingham and Bristol. The engine had the distinction of hauling the train carrying Sir Winston Churchill from Liverpool on his return from the North Atlantic Treaty talks with President Roosevelt in the USA in 1942. No 45593 was transferred to Leeds Holbeck on March 23, 1965 and mainly worked rail tours. It was also given a yellow cab side warning stripe to indicate it was not allowed to work the West Coast Main Line south of Crewe where it was out-of-gauge. *Kolhapur* was withdrawn in October 1967 and purchased in January of the following year by the then Standard Gauge Steam Trust. Photograph taken by Geoff Warnes on April 22, 1967.

Above CUDWORTH

Ivatt Class 2MT 2-6-2T locomotive no. 41282 is with a 'push-and-pull' train at Cudworth on June 7, 1958. The view is facing south east. The locomotive will go forward and turn off at Cudworth south junction for Barnsley via Monk Bretton. Services between Cudworth and Barnsley Court House ceased two days later. Built at Crewe Works no. 41282 was in service between October 1950 and November 1963. The photograph was taken by Geoff Warnes whilst the engine was allocated to Royston.

Opposite top CONISBROUGH VIADUCT

A one coach 'push-and-pull' is heading across the Conisbrough viaduct, carrying the Dearne Valley Railway on September 8, 1951. Two days later, this passenger service linking the 20¼ miles between Wakefield (Kirkgate) and Edlington-for-Balby was withdrawn, having been in operation since 1912. The viaduct's designer was W. Kaye, of Leeds, and John Steel was the clerk of works on behalf of Messrs Lovat. Steel was widely experienced in large engineering contracts but regarded Conisbrough viaduct as the largest structure he had seen in the way of railway bridge building. Stretching from the picturesque Conisbrough Cliffs to Cadeby, the total length of the viaduct was 528 yards. It was estimated that no less than 15,000,000 bricks were used in the construction and 250 men were employed. Photograph by Geoffrey Oates.

Opposite below CUDWORTH

The 16.10 Leeds City – Sheffield stopping train hauled by Compound Class 4P 4-4-0 locomotive no. 41154 arrives at Cudworth station on July 24, 1951. The view is looking north, along the former Midland main line; the Midland Railway opened the resited Cudworth station in 1854. The Hull & Barnsley Railway – whose lines may be seen to the right – also ran passenger services into Cudworth station from July 27, 1885. The H&B had its own platform connected to the main station by a long footbridge. Closure of the station occurred on January 1, 1968. No 41154 was in service between September 1925 to July 1955. Photograph by Ben Brooksbank.

Above DENABY MAIN COLLIERY
Beyer-Peacock 0-6-0ST locomotive, NCB no. 7 and named *Warmsworth* (later renamed *Conisbro*) was built in 1896. It is working from the washery to the boat staithes. The photograph was taken by Geoff Warnes on February 18, 1961.

Opposite top DARTON STATION
The line through Darton was promoted in 1846 by the Sheffield, Rotherham, Barnsley, Wakefield, Huddersfield & Goole Railway. Darton station opened on January 1, 1850. Stone setts were still an attractive feature at the station when Class 2MT 2-6-2T locomotive no. 41253 called with an afternoon service from Wakefield Kirkgate to Barnsley Exchange in November 1955. Unlike a number of stations in the area Darton is still open. Crewe Works-built no. 41253 was withdrawn from Lancaster Green Ayre in May 1964 after nearly 14 years and five months in service. Photograph by W.A. Camwell.

Opposite below DANBY WISKE
Hurtling through Danby Wiske and picking up water from the troughs is Class V2 2-6-2 locomotive no. 976. Although pictured in May 1948 the engine still has its LNER number but would eventually carry no. 60976. Allocated from new in 1943 to York (North), the locomotive was withdrawn from St Margarets in October 1965. Photograph courtesy of *Yorkshire Post Newspapers*.

Above DENABY MAIN LEVEL CROSSING

Heading west with a coal train through Denaby Main level crossing is Class O4 2-8-0 locomotive no. 63704. In the background is Denaby Main colliery which existed between c. 1863-1968 and the site is now cleared. No. 63704 was withdrawn from Retford Thrumpton during March 1963 after 44 years 5 months in service, being subsequently scrapped at Doncaster Works. Photograph taken on March 11, 1961 by Geoff Warnes.

Opposite top DONCASTER WORKS

Doncaster Works was established in the town by the Great Northern Railway in 1853 and over the years built many noted engines, as well as carriage sets and wagons. Amongst the locomotives are *Flying Scotsman* and *Mallard*, both of which are still extant even today. A significant proportion of the Works has been demolished and waits redevelopment while a section of the original area still thrives under the private ownership of Wabtec Rail Ltd. Class J39 0-6-0 locomotive no. 64970 has met a sad end at Doncaster Works – the dismantling area for countless steam locomotives – on June 4, 1961. Entering traffic from Darlington Works in August 1938, the engine was withdrawn from Retford Thrumpton in May 1961. Photograph by Ron Fisher.

Opposite below DONCASTER

Viewed from Doncaster's North Bridge, Class O4 2-8-0 locomotive no. 63893 heads an 'Up' train on the approach to the town's station. Lines north of the station provide routes to Leeds, Edinburgh and Hull. In the distance is an 'Avoiding Line' – a route to enable rail traffic to by-pass the railway station area when heading west or east. No. 63893 was built at NBLC and in service between 1919 and 1965. Withdrawn from Langwith Junction, the engine was scrapped at T.W. Ward (Beighton). Photographed on February 8, 1963 by Geoff Warnes.

DONCASTER

Looking north from Hexthorpe Bridge, Doncaster, towards the town's station, no fewer than four V2 Class 2-6-2 locomotives may be seen in this view taken on September 7, 1958. Identified are nos 60885 and 60930. The first locomotive was allocated to Copley Hill (Leeds) at this time and the second one to Doncaster. They were withdrawn in 1963 and 1962 respectively. A station was opened at Doncaster on September 7, 1848 and replaced to the north during September 1850. Photograph by Geoff Warnes.

Above and below DONCASTER

Gresley Hunt Class 4-4-0 locomotive no. 62701 *Derbyshire* has been photographed on two separate occasions in the same location. The top picture dates from June 13, 1959 and the one below, August 15, 1959. A month later the locomotive was withdrawn from Hull Botanic Gardens after spending nearly 32 years in service. Both photographs were taken by Geoff Warnes.

DONCASTER CARR LOCOMOTIVE SHED

Situated a mile south of Doncaster station, Doncaster Carr locomotive shed opened in March 1876. Built of brick, the facility contained 12 roads and space for approx. 100 engines. Riddles-designed Britannia Class 4–6–2 locomotive no. 70038 *Robin Hood* was photographed at the shed by Bill Reed on May 15 1959. Built at Crewe Works and entering service in January 1953, the locomotive was allocated to Norwich Thorpe at the time of the picture. Following withdrawal in August 1967, no 70038 was scrapped at J. McWilliams (Shettleston).

Above DONCASTER STATION

A night shot taken on February 16, 1967 finds Stanier 'Black Five' 4-6-0 locomotive no. 45208 at platform 3 at Doncaster station at the front of a parcels train from Bradford. Entering service during November 1935, no. 45208 was only months away from withdrawal in October 1967. The last allocation was Low Moor. Photograph by Geoff Warnes.

Below DONCASTER SHED

Located just north of the main Doncaster shed is Class K3 2-6-0 locomotive no. 61964. After just over 25 years in service the engine was withdrawn from Doncaster in July 1961. Photograph by Bill Reed.

Above DONCASTER SHED

Facing north, two locomotives pictured at the north end of the shed are Class B16 4-6-0 no. 61439 and Class A3 4-6-2 no. 60038 *Firdaussi*. In the post-war years neither engine was allocated to Doncaster. Photograph by Bill Reed.

Below DONCASTER SHED

Replaced c. 1926 by a new 500-ton mechanical coaler, Doncaster's north coaling stage – to the left behind the locomotive – was subsequently retained as a stand-by. Gresley Class O2 2-8-0 locomotive no. 63939 built at Doncaster in 1923 had several stints at Doncaster shed before withdrawal in September 1963. Photograph by Bill Reed.

Above DONCASTER

With Doncaster station, a K3 and a V2 locomotive in the background, Class 9F 2-10-0 locomotive no. 92057 heads west on the 'Sheffield line' during May 1956. At this time the Crewe works-built engine had only been in service seven months and would be withdrawn after working just under ten years in October 1965. Photograph by Geoff Warnes.

Below DONCASTER STATION

Doncaster station was rebuilt in 1938 and the work included the construction of the present frontage. Stanier Jubilee Class 4-6-0 locomotive no. 45739 *Ulster* has just eased into Platform 1 on April 13, 1966. The engine had only nine months left in service, being withdrawn in January 1967, after a little over 30 years in existence. Photograph by Geoff Warnes.

Above DUNFORD BRIDGE STATION

Opened by the Manchester, Sheffield & Lincolnshire Railway on July 14, 1845, Dunford Bridge station was close to the two eastern portals of Woodhead Tunnel. When a new tunnel was created, a few yards to the south of the older ones, to accommodate electrification of the line, Dunford Bridge station was resited and opened on June 14 1954. Closure came on January 5, 1970 and no trace remains of either the old or new station. Class B1 4-6-0 locomotive is working on the 09.00 from Manchester (London Road) to Sheffield (Victoria) on July 25, 1951. Entering service from the NBLC in August 1957, the engine was allocated to Gorton at the time of the picture, being withdrawn from Sheffield Darnall in September 1962. Photograph by Ben Brooksbank.

Opposite top DORE & TOTLEY

Taken from Twentywell Lane Bridge, the view is looking north to Dore & Totley station. Opened by the Midland Railway as Dore & Totley, the station was renamed Dore in 1971. In later years the island and eastern platforms were removed, but the name Dore & Totley was restored in April 2008. Built by Neilson, Reid & Co., Class 2P 4-4-0 locomotive no. 40556 is working a train to Manchester on October 9, 1954. Photograph by Geoff Warnes.

Opposite below DUNFORD BRIDGE RAILWAY STATION

The photograph was taken facing east, along the ex-Great Central Manchester – Sheffield line, with the locomotive about to enter the Woodhead Tunnel at Dunford Bridge station. Taken during July 1951, the photograph predates electrification of the line. Work on the scheme had begun before the Second World War but was postponed on the commencement of hostilities. A new start was subsequently made but the originally proposed link to Manchester Central, the Docks and the Trafford Park industrial area was abandoned. Built by the NBLC, Class O4 2-8-0 locomotive no. 63749 was in service between November 1917 and October 1959, being withdrawn from Staveley. Photograph by Ben Brooksbank.

Below EDLINGTON HALT

Opened by the Dearne Valley Railway on June 3, 1912, the Halt was titled Edlington for Balby (Doncaster). Like others on the DVR, Edlington consisted of a bed of sleepers at track level with an old coach body for a waiting shelter. A Hughes-designed railmotor originally operated on the passenger services and was fitted with vacuum operated retractable steps. Crewe Works-built Class 2MT 2-6-2T locomotive no. 41283 was allocated to Wakefield when new in November 1950. Thereafter, the engine moved further afield, and was withdrawn from Templecombe in July 1965. Edlington Halt is depicted here by Geoffrey Oates during June 1951; abandonment of passenger services occurred on September 10, 1951.

Above EMLEY MOOR COLLIERY
Built by Hudswell Clarke (works no. 1817) in 1953, 0-4-0ST locomotive *Standback no. 3* was supplied new to Hartley Bank colliery, near Wakefield and transferred to Emley Moor on February 6, 1968. It is seen here on August 6, 1971 and was scrapped on site during 1976 by Roe Brothers & Co. Ltd of Rotherham. Rail traffic ended at Emley Moor in July 1982 and the pit was closed shortly after the ending of the 1984/85 Miners' Strike. Photograph by Bill Reed.

Opposite Top EDLINGTON YORKSHIRE MAIN COLLIERY
Built by Hudswell Clarke in 1916 (works no. 1178) 0-6-0ST locomotive no. 18 *Eddie* was formerly ex- Appleby-Froddingham Steel Co. Ltd, Scunthorpe before transfer to Edlington in June 1950. Photographed by John Law c. 1969, the locomotive was scrapped by March 1972. The colliery existed between 1911 – 1985.

Above ELSECAR JUNCTION

Elsecar junction, situated some distance from Elsecar, was on the now defunct Woodhead Line and near to the Wath marshalling yard – out of view. Robinson Class O4 2-8-0 locomotive no. 63898 was photographed at Elsecar Junction, by Geoff Warnes on February 18, 1961. At this time no. 63898 was allocated to Mexborough shed a short distance from the area here. Introduced in June 1919, the engine was withdrawn from Frodingham in May 1963. The line through Elsecar Junction, along with Wath marshalling yard, closed in 1988.

Above **FIRBECK**

Class O4 2-8-0 locomotive no. 63647 is depicted working in the Firbeck colliery area. The colliery existed between c. 1925 and 1968. Photograph taken on March 24, 1962 by Geoff Warnes.

Below **GOOLE**

LMS 0-6-0T 3F Jinties 47581, 47634, 47438, 47589 and 47462 are stored at Goole MPD with L&YR Class 21 0-4-0ST 51222 in the summer of 1960. Photograph by Keith Platt.

Above GOOLE

Nicknamed 'Pugs', the L&YR Class 21 was a group of small 0-4-0ST locomotives built by the company for shunting duties. They were designed by J.A.F. Aspinall and the L&YR employed them for operation in the industrial areas and docks of Fleetwood, Goole, Liverpool and Salford. Later they were more widely dispersed. No. 51222 is pictured in the Goole docks area during August 1960. Built by Horwich Works, the engine entered service in December 1901 and was withdrawn from Goole during March 1962. Photograph courtesy of Colourrail.

Opposite top GRASSINGTON & THRESHFIELD

The 'morning' goods arrives at Grassington & Threshfield terminus behind Class 4F 0-6-0 locomotive no. 43999 in the summer of 1959. This Skipton-based loco was a regular performer on the branch, although arrival could often be delayed if the crew saw mushrooms growing in fields close to the line! No 43999 was withdrawn from Skipton in May 1965 after over 44 years in service. Grassington station, a single storey building, was opened by the Yorkshire Dales Railway on July 29, 1902 (the official opening date is 30th July 1902 but four public trains ran the previous day). Threshfield was added soon afterwards. The station was the terminus of the 8.75 mile long Grassington Branch Line and was actually situated in Threshfield. Closure to passengers occurred on September 22, 1930 but it continued to be popular with excursion traffic until the 1960s. The last such excursion was operated in 1969 by the then Embsay & Grassington Railway Preservation Society. Complete closure was affected on August 11 1969. The station area was subsequently cleared and redeveloped. A new road – Piece Fields – presently occupies the old site. Photograph by David Joy.

Opposite below GRASSINGTON & THRESHFIELD

Another shot of Class 4F 0-6-0 locomotive no. 43999 at Grassington & Threshfield shows the engine in charge of shunting operations in 1959. At the time of the Grasington Branch line opening, passenger services were operated by the Midland Railway and later the LMS. The fine array of signals includes two Midland Railway lower quadrants. Today, part of the southern end of the Grassington Branch still exists and provides access to Swinden limeworks. Photograph by David Joy.

Above GREAT HORTON STATION

The Queensbury lines linking Bradford, Halifax and Keighley were among the most spectacularly engineered in Yorkshire. They were also some of the least profitable – a situation not helped by their stations built on the grand scale. There was little sign of life when Class N1 0-6-2T locomotive no. 69442 called at Great Horton station situated on the line from Bradford to Thornton via Queensbury. The station was opened on October 14, 1878 by the Great Northern Railway. Closure to passengers was brought into effect on May 13, 1955 and complete closure occurred on June 28, 1965. The area was then cleared and redeveloped. No. 69442 is still fitted with condensing gear for working underground lines in the London area and was withdrawn from Bradford Hammerton Street shed during September 1953 after more than 43 years in service. Photograph by W.A. Camwell.

Opposite top GLASSHOUGHTON

Hunslet supplied 0-6-0T locomotive S118 to Glasshoughton colliery in 1953 and it survived until April 1973. The photograph was taken by Bill Reed in May 1972. Closure for the colliery came in 1986.

Opposite below HARROGATE STARBECK SHED

Harrogate Starbeck shed was built by the NER in 1857, extended four times between 1865 and 1889, then rebuilt by BR in 1956, until finally being demolished c. 1962. Class 4P 2-6-2T locomotive no. 42477 existed between 1937 – 1965. Photograph by Bill Reed.

Above **HALIFAX DRYCLOUGH JUNCTION**

Halifax's position in a narrow tributary valley of Calderdale did not lend itself to easy rail access. The first line into the town from Greetland, opened in 1844, had gradients as steep as 1 in 44 and many freight trains required banking assistance until the end of steam. Ex-L&YR Class 27 0-6-0 locomotive no. 52515 is engaged in such duties at Dryclough Junction in June 1962. In the foreground are the tracks of the later line from Sowerby Bridge through Copley. Built at Horwich Works and entering service in November 1906, no. 52515 was withdrawn from Sowerby Bridge in December 1962. Photograph by Arthur R. Wilson.

Opposite top **HARROGATE STARBECK SHED**

Gresley Class D49 4-4-0 locomotive no. 62759 *The Craven* was built at Darlington in August 1934. The engine was allocated to Harrogate Starbeck from December 1954, and withdrawal from Hull Dairycoates occurred in January 1961. Photograph by Bill Reed.

Opposite below **HARROGATE STARBECK SHED**

The locomotives seen here include WD 'Austerity' Class 2-8-0 no. 90054 and two Gresley Class J39 0-6-0 locomotives, nos 64942 and 64944. The WD survived until 1967, the two J39s, 1962. Photograph by Bill Reed.

Below HOLMFIELD STATION

Class N1 0-6-2T locomotive no. 69484 is depicted leaving Holmfield on May 21, 1955. It was the last day of passenger services from Halifax to Bradford (Exchange) and Keighley via Queensbury. Largely duplicating existing routes, these lines stood little chance of competing with bus services and then motorcars. Holmfield station was originally opened by the Halifax & Ovenden Joint Railway on December 12, 1879. Boasting extensive goods facilities, to serve nearby woollen mills, Holmfield also had a 10 ton crane and at one time provided sidings for Drakes Ltd and Shell Mex Ltd. At Holmfield, trains reversed on to the Halifax High Level branch providing the opportunity for passengers to interchange for journeys on to Keighley. The station closed completely on June 27, 1960 and once the station area was cleared, the site was redeveloped. Built at Doncaster Works and entering service during June 1912, no. 69484 was withdrawn from Ardsley in September 1957. Photograph from the David Joy collection.

Above HELLIFIELD STATION

The first Hellifield station was opened by the 'Little' North Western Railway on July 30, 1849 but resited to the north by the Midland Railway, June 1, 1880. Following a large cash injection from British Rail in association with English Heritage and the Railway Heritage Trust, the station was refurbished in 1994/1995. Further work was carried out in 2013. Pictured at Hellifield, on April 16, 1960 is Johnson Class 3F 0-6-0 locomotive no. 43585. Completed in October 1899, the engine spent almost 63 years in service before withdrawal from Hellifield in November 1962. Photograph by Geoff Warnes.

Above HUDDERSFIELD STATION

Designed by architect James Pigott Pritchett, Huddersfield station was opened on August 3 1847 by the London & North Western Railway Co. With a classical-style facade featuring a portico of the Corinthian order, six columns in width and two in depth, the station was described by John Betjeman as the most splendid in England. Sir Nikolaus Pevsner agreed, adding: 'one of the best early railway stations in England'. Jubilee Class 4-6-0 locomotive no. 45562 *Alberta* is about to leave a bay platform with a parcels train to Leeds. Erected by the NBLC in August 1934, the engine was one of the last two Jubilees in service being withdrawn from Leeds Holbeck during October 1967. Scrapping occurred in May 1968 at Cashmore's, Great Bridge. The photograph was taken on July 13, 1966 by Patrick O'Brien.

Below HUDDERSFIELD SHED

'Black Five' Class 4-6-0 locomotive no. 44763 is at Huddersfield shed on March 24, 1963. The depot, existing from 1882 and altered in 1905, closed on January 2, 1967. Photograph courtesy of Peter Sedge.

Above HORTON-IN-RIBBLESDALE STATION

Opened as Horton on May 1, 1876, the station was renamed Horton-in-Ribblesdale on September 26, 1927. Closing to goods on February 2, 1965, and passengers May 4, 1970 the station still took occasional excursion traffic until reopening on July 14, 1986. Storming through during March 1963 is Jubilee Class 4-6-0 locomotive no. 45739 *Ulster*, in service December 1936 to January 1967. Photograph courtesy of *Yorkshire Post Newspapers*.

Below HEXTHORPE JUNCTION

At Hexthorpe junction Crewe Works-built Standard Class 7 4-6-2 locomotive no. 70037 *Hereward the Wake* is heading west from the Avoiding Line with a petrol train. The engine was in service between December 1952 to November 1966. Photograph taken c.1962 by David Thorpe.

Above HULL PARAGON

Gresley Class A3 4-6-2 locomotive no. 60080 *Dick Turpin* is at Hull Paragon station. The engine was erected by the NBLC in November 1924 as an A1 and rebuilt to A3 in November 1942. *Dick Turpin* was at a Leeds shed between 1960 and 1963 and was withdrawn from Gateshead in October 1964. Photograph by Bill Reed.

Below HULL DRAPER'S YARD

An identified B1 is cut up at Draper's yard in 1965. Photograph by Rev. J. David Benson and reproduced courtesy of the A1 Steam Locomotive Trust.

Above HULL DRAPER'S YARD

Peppercorn Class A1 4-6-2 locomotive no. 60157 *Great Eastern* meets a sorry end at Draper's yard, Neptune Street, Hull. Built at Doncaster Works, no. 60157 entered service on November 3, 1949 but was not named until November 1951. Withdrawal occurred on January 10, 1965. Photograph by Rev. J. David Benson and reproduced courtesy of the A1 Steam Locomotive Trust.

Below HULL

Gresley Class V3 2-6-2T locomotive no. 67682 was sent from Blaydon to Hull Botanic Gardens in January 1959, and moved to Hull Dairycoates five months later, returning north-east to Darlington in November 1961. Erected at Doncaster, the locomotive entered service in September 1939 and was withdrawn in September 1963. No. 67682 was photographed near Hull Paragon station by Bill Reed.

Above HULL

Photographed from Hull's Hessle Road flyover, WD 'Austerity' 2-8-0 locomotive no. 90262 is working a mineral 'empties' train from Alexandra Dock to Dairycoates c. 1964. Built at NBLC in October 1943, the engine was allocated to Hull Dairycoates shed in November 1963 and remained there until withdrawal in June 1967. It was cut up at Draper's yard in the city by January 1968. Photograph courtesy of Colourrail.

Opposite top HULL DAIRYCOATES SHED

Opening in 1863, the shed eventually comprised six brick built roundhouses, a three track shed and another with two tracks. Closure to steam occurred on June 24, 1967 and then completely on September 21, 1970. WD 'Austerity' Class 2-8-0 locomotive no. 90623 was allocated to Dairycoates 1958-1961; Class 4MT 2-6-0 no. 43078, 1950-1965; Class B1 4-6-0 no. 61010 *Wildebeeste*, 1959 -1965. Photograph reproduced courtesy of Colourrail.

Opposite below HULL

Class J39 0-6-0 locomotive no. 64943 is seen near Hull Alexandra Dock on February 29 1960. The engine was with withdrawn from Hull Dairycoates in December 1962 after over 24 years in service. Reproduced courtesy of Colourrail.

Below KIRKSTALL

On June 24 1952 'Black Five' Class 4-6-0 locomotive no. 44658 has just scurried through Kirkstall station on its way from Leeds to Bradford with an evening commuter train. Built at Crewe Works and entering service at the end of May 1949, the locomotive was withdrawn from Springs Branch (Wigan) during November 1967. Opened in July 1846 by the Leeds & Bradford Railway, Kirkstall station was rebuilt in 1905 for route widening and closed on March 22, 1965. Photograph courtesy of *Yorkshire Post Newspapers*.

Above KILDWICK

Hauling a Leeds-Morecambe train at Kildwick's Skipton Road level crossing – between Keighley and Skipton – is 'Black Five' Class 4-6-0 locomotive no. 45040. Built at Vulcan Foundry, no. 45040 entered traffic during October 1935 and withdrawal from Crewe South was implemented during July 1967. The line between Shipley and Colne was originally opened by the Leeds & Bradford Extension Railway; the section between Keighley to Skipton opened on March 16, 1847. Kildwick station opened in April 1848 and later became Kildwick for/& Cross Hills. Resited 16 chains further west on April 7 1889, the station closed on March 22 1965. Looking east towards Leeds the photograph is reproduced courtesy of *Yorkshire Post Newspapers*.

Above **LEEDS HOLBECK**

Bounded by Bridge Road, Nineveh Road and Sweet Street West, Holbeck shed comprising two roundhouses was opened on May 9, 1868. Including a repair shop, ramped coal stage and water tank, the shed later had a mechanical coaler with two bunkers. It closed on October 2, 1967 and the area was subsequently cleared. 'Black Five' Class 4-6-0 locomotive no. 45001 is beneath the Holbeck coaler on January 8, 1967. Emerging from Crewe Works during April 1935, the engine was allocated to Carnforth at the time of the photograph and was withdrawn from there in March 1968. Photograph by Geoff Warnes.

Opposite top **LEEDS CITY STATION**

Fairburn Class 4P 2-6-4T locomotive no. 42699 is near Leeds City station, out of view to the right, on September 4, 1965. To service from Derby Works during October 1945, the engine was allocated to several Scottish sheds, Polmadie, Motherwell and Dumfries, until a return south to Leeds Neville Hill transpired in October 1963. Moving to Leeds Holbeck in June 1966, no. 42699 was withdrawn from there in May 1967. Following the amalgamation of Leeds Wellington and Leeds New stations Leeds City station was opened on May 2, 1938. A major refurbishment of the building was completed on May 1, 1967 and included a new concourse, platforms, roof and car park. Photograph by Geoff Warnes.

Opposite bottom **LEEDS CITY STATION**

Following the Leeds City 1967 refurbishment, the new roof, as seen here, was deemed to be too low, allowing in little natural light. Provisions for future trends in passenger movements were also considered inadequate. Therefore, a major refurbishment took place between 1999-2002. This saw a new, higher roof erected and some of the old Wellington platforms, which had been turned over to parcels use, re-employed for passenger trains in addition to new platforms being constructed to the south. 'Black Five' Class 4-6-0 locomotive no. 44951 was photographed by Geoff Warnes on September 4, 1965. Allocated to Mirfield at this time, no. 44951 was withdrawn from Wakefield in December 1966.

LEEDS COPLEY HILL

West of Leeds Central station and located in the triangle formed by the Leeds Central, Armley Moor and Ardsley lines, Leeds Copley Hill engine shed was formerly owned by the Great Northern Railway and opened in 1900. It had five through roads, a ramped coal stage, water tank and turntable. Re-roofed c. 1949, the shed closed on September 7, 1964 and the site was cleared. Peppercorn Class A1 4-6-2 locomotive no. 60139 *Sea Eagle* emerged from Darlington Works in December 1948 but was not named until May 1950. Allocated to Leeds Copley Hill between July 1951 and December 1955, the engine was withdrawn from Doncaster in June 1964 and sold for scrap in January 1965 to Cox & Danks, Wadsley Bridge. Photograph courtesy of *Yorkshire Post Newspapers*.

Above LEEDS MARSH LANE

Taken on November 20, 1951, the photograph shows Marsh Lane box, Wesley Place above right and the west end of Marsh Lane cutting. Out of view to the left was a goods station. The lines in the foreground form part of the Leeds – Selby route, one of Britain's first main lines, opening in 1834. The new railway speeded up travel between the two points. Stagecoaches during previous summers carried weekly around 400 passengers. By comparison the summer of 1835 saw 3,500 people travel by rail. Class J77 0-6-0T locomotive no. 68436 entered traffic from Gateshead at the end of October 1900. At the time of the photograph, the engine was allocated to Leeds Neville Hill but was withdrawn from Tweedmouth in June 1956 and cut up at Darlington Works. Photograph courtesy of *Yorkshire Post Newspapers*.

Below LEEDS HOLBECK

A scene at Leeds Holbeck shed on January 8, 1967 shows the labour intensive work involved in maintaining a steam locomotive. In October of the same year the shed would close to steam. To serve diesel locomotives, the Holbeck repair shop was turned into a depot and a servicing facility was also added a little later. The no. 1 type concrete coaling tower, seen on the right, could hold 300 tons of coal and service two locomotives at a time. It was demolished along with other buildings in 1970. Unfortunately, both the diesel-electric Class 44 and the steam locomotive are unidentified. Photograph by Geoff Warnes.

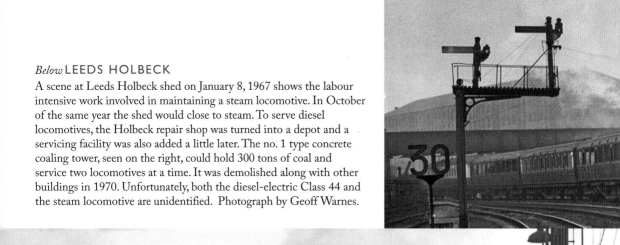

Above **LEEDS MARSH LANE**

Class B1 4-6-0 locomotive no. 61020 *Gemsbok* heads a Leeds – Hull train past a J77 0-6-0T locomotive on November 20, 1951. The photograph was taken on the same day as the one on page 71 but this time the camera is pointing west towards a footbridge, linking Railway Street with Shannon Street. A Goods station yard is to the right of the J77. Adjacent, at one time, was the Leeds & Selby Railway's Marsh Lane station opened on September 22, 1834 and closed April 1, 1869. Darlington Works-built no. 61020, entering traffic in February 1947, was allocated to York (North) at the time of the photograph. Subsequent years saw the engine return to the depot twice, being withdrawn from there in November 1962. Scrapping took place at Darlington two months later. Photograph courtesy of *Yorkshire Post Newspapers*.

Above LEEDS CENTRAL STATION

A temporary terminus, erected in Wellington Street and named Leeds Central, opened on September 18, 1848, and was gradually developed over the ensuing nine years. It was jointly owned by the Great Northern, Lancashire & Yorkshire, North Eastern and London & North Western Railways. In time, the latter two companies switched allegiance to the Midland-owned Wellington station and subsequently built their own station known as Leeds New. Central station closed on April 29, 1967 and was demolished; services were diverted to Leeds City. Ivatt Class N1 0-6-2T locomotive no. 69440 was photographed by Geoff Warnes at Leeds Central on June 22, 1953. Completed at Doncaster Works in February 1908 the engine was one of 56 in the Class ordered in six batches between January 1907 and September 1911. At the outset, many N1s were allocated to the London area but large numbers were later moved to the West Riding. They worked passenger services between Leeds, Bradford and Wakefield and often operated as station pilots at Wakefield and Leeds. They were superseded by Gresley's N2s. Withdrawal for no. 69440 came from Ardsley in March 1957.

Opposite above LEEDS CITY

Class 4P 2-6-4T locomotive no. 42251 is ready to leave Leeds City station at 09.25, on August 29, 1967, with a train for Bradford. Photograph by Bill Wright.

Opposite below LEEDS HOLBECK

Another batch of locomotives seen at Leeds Holbeck include: Class 4P 2-6-4T locomotive no. 42622; Jubilee Class 4-6-0 no. 45647 *Sturdee*; Class 8F 2-8-0 no. 48283; and 'Black Five' Class 4-6-0 no. 44988. Photograph taken in January 1967 and reproduced courtesy of John Law.

LEEDS HOLBECK

Positioned around a Leeds Holbeck shed turntable are the following locomotives: Standard Class 5 4-6-0 no. 73103, built at Doncaster Works and in service between September 1955 and October 1965; Ivatt Class 4 2-6-0 no. 43130, built at Horwich Works and in steam between October 1951 and July 1967; Class B1 4-6-0 no. 61121, erected by the NBLC and extant between January 1947 and April 1966; Class 5 4-6-0 no. 45204, built by Armstrong Whitworth in November 1935 and in service until January 1967. Photograph taken on August 1, 1965 by Bill Wright.

Above and below MANVERS COLLIERY

Two Manvers locomotives are seen on a line that linked both Manvers and Barnburgh collieries. The top picture shows Manvers 41 *Elsie*; the one below an unidentified J94. Dearne Junction signal box is visible in both views. Manvers colliery closed during March 1988 and the Coal Preparation Plant a year later. Photographs taken on March 3, 1966 by Geoff Warnes.

Above MARSDEN

'Black Five' Class 4-6-0 locomotive no. 45063 is approaching Standedge Tunnel whilst working the 16.00 Hull to Liverpool Lime Street (via Manchester Exchange station) on April 8, 1960. No. 45063 emerged from Vulcan Foundry in December 1935 and remained in service until October 1966. Photograph taken, looking east along the former LNW Manchester – Leeds main line, by Ben Brooksbank.

Opposite top LITTLE WEIGHTON

Pictured at Little Weighton station, and heading west with a passenger service, is Class 0-4-4T locomotive no. 67337 on the old Hull & Barnsley line. The station was opened on July 27, 1885 – a week after the line. Closure to passengers occurred on August 1 1955, and completely July 6, 1964. Completed at Darlington Works during June 1901, the locomotive was withdrawn from Middlesbrough in March 1957. Photograph reproduced courtesy of Nicholas Cox.

Opposite below MANNINGHAM

A brick-built square shed featuring a triple gable roof was opened at Manningham by the Midland Railway in 1872. Closure came on April 30, 1967. Amongst the identified locomotives pictured at the shed on January 8, 1967 are: Class 4MT 2-6-0 no. 43117, completed at Horwich Works June 1951 and withdrawn July 1967; Class 4MT 2-6-0 no. 43096 built at Darlington Works December 1950 and survived until November 1967; and Class 4P 2-6-4T no. 42093, built at Brighton Works and in service May 1951 – October 1967. Photograph taken by Geoff Warnes.

Above and below MEXBOROUGH SHED

Two engine sheds preceded the one that was opened at Mexborough in 1875 by the Great Central Railway. A dead end shed, it included 15 roads, a coal stage, water tank and 60ft turntable. Locomotives were supplied from Mexborough mainly for coal trains and for a period they were in great demand at Wath marshalling yard. The LNER Garratt was also stabled at Mexborough shed, which was closed in February 1964. The top picture of Class N4 0-6-2T locomotive no. 69308, at Mexborough, was taken in June 1959, the one below showing a broad view of the depot in August 1959. Both pictures by Geoff Warnes.

Above MILLHOUSES

Deeley Class 3F 0-6-0 locomotive no. 43775 is working a goods train through Millhouses, located on the Midland main line, on August 21, 1954. The engine was withdrawn just over a year later after over 52 years in service. Photograph by Geoff Warnes.

Below MEXBOROUGH WEST JUNCTION

The view is north west with Manvers Main colliery in the background and Class J6 0-6-0 locomotive no. 4174 (later 64174) is hauling a train of empty wagons on the approach to Mexborough West Junction. Completed at Doncaster Works in October 1911, the engine was withdrawn from Retford in September 1961. The photograph was taken on April 28 1950 by Ben Brooksbank.

Above and below MIRFIELD SHED

Two earlier sheds existed at Mirfield before the Lancashire & Yorkshire Railway opened a third in 1885. Including eight roads, a ramped coal stage, turntable and water tank, the facility was re-roofed in 1934 and closed in April 1967. Both pictures - taken by Geoff Warnes on December 17, 1966 - show two different views of 'Black Five' Class 4-6-0 locomotive no. 45109 and Class 8F 2-8-0 locomotive no. 48320.

Above MIRFIELD

The view is facing east towards Mirfield station with Mirfield engine shed out of sight to the left. Class 8F 2-8-0 locomotive no. 48146, heading west, has passed another 8F, no. 48095, travelling in the opposite direction. The shed's ramped coaling stage may be seen off-centre to the right. Photograph taken on June 26, 1964 by Ben Brooksbank.

Below MIRFIELD STATION

Easing a train of empty coal wagons eastwards through Mirfield station is Class 8F 2-8-0 locomotive no. 48676. Opened by the Manchester & Leeds Railway in April 1845, the station was resited on March 5, 1866. No. 48676, built at Brighton Works, was allocated to Lancashire sheds for all its working life – April 1944 to October 1967. Photograph taken on July 29, 1966 by Ben Brooksbank.

Above NEWMARKET COLLIERY

Newmarket colliery was sunk by the Fenton Brothers in 1837 and closed in 1983. The colliery and sidings were to be found east of Stanley station. Lines also extended to a staith at Cringleworth, spoil heaps and a junction at Royds Green Lower. Rail traffic ceased in 1981. Built by Hunslet in 1935, 0-6-0ST *Jubilee* was ex-Waterloo Main colliery before arriving at Newmarket in July 1966. Photographed by Bill Reed on September 16, 1971, the engine was scrapped on site by Wakefield Metal Traders Ltd during March 1973.

Opposite top NEWLAY & HORSFORTH STATION

A train headed by 'Crab' Class 2-6-0 locomotive no. 42926 is moving eastwards on the old Leeds & Bradford Railway, and through Newlay & Horsforth station on June 26, 1964. The station was opened on September 1, 1846 as Newlay, becoming Newlay for Horsforth, April 1, 1875; Newlay & Horsforth October 4, 1889; and Newlay June 12, 1961. Closure came on March 22 1965. No. 42926 was in service between May 1931 and October 1964. Photograph by Ben Brooksbank.

Opposite below NEWMARKET COLLIERY

Built by Hunslet in 1943, 0-6-0ST *Jess* was at Waterloo Main colliery before arrival at Newmarket in November 1968. Photographed by Bill Reed on September 16, 1971, *Jess* was scrapped on site in November 1973.

Above **NORMANTON**

Peppercorn Class A1 4-6-2 locomotive no. 60146 *Peregrine* passes Normanton shed with a Healey Mills – York freight in April 1965. Emerging from Darlington Works in April 1949, the engine was named in December 1950. The allocation from new was to Doncaster followed by moves to Copley Hill (Leeds), York (North), Neville Hill, York(North) from where it was withdrawn on October 4, 1965. The last recorded passenger train worked by no. 60146 was the 09.42 Newcastle to Liverpool on March 3, 1965; the last parcels, May 28, 1965 and the final goods, June 4, 1965. After languishing at York for a period, *Peregrine* was sold for scrap in November 1965 to T.W. Ward of Killamarsh. Photograph by Roger Bastin, reproduced courtesy of the A1 Steam Locomotive Trust.

Below NORMANTON

Goosehill Junction, Normanton with Peppercorn Class A1 4-6-2 locomotive no. 60145 *Saint Mungo* fronting a Healey Mills to Tyne Yard freight train. Built at Darlington Works in March 1949, the engine was named in August 1950. Allocated to Gateshead when new, this was followed by stints at Copley Hill, Leeds; York (North); Darlington; and York (North) from where it was withdrawn in June 1966.

The final recorded working is on 19th April 1966 when it hauled the 3.50 am York-Stockton passenger train; pulled a parcels to Sunderland; ran light engine to Heaton and returned to York on a newspaper empties train. The engine was the last A1 in service and there was a brave attempt by Geoff Drury to save it but this failed. *Saint Mungo* was sold for scrap to A. Draper in August 1966 and cut up a month later. Photograph taken in May 1965 by Roger Bastin and reproduced by courtesy of the A1 Steam Locomotive Trust.

Above OAKENSHAW NORTH JUNCTION

Taken from Doncaster Road bridge, the view is looking towards Oakenshaw North Junction and the signal box. The tracks on the left lead to Snydale and Normanton, the ones on the right to Crofton and on to Pontefract Tanshelf and Monkhill. WD 'Austerity' Class locomotive 2-8-0 no. 90268 is heading a train on May 16, 1959. Completed at the NBLC in October 1945 the engine was withdrawn from Hull Dairycoates in November 1963. Photograph taken by Geoff Warnes.

Opposite top NORMANTON

In a view facing north east, Normanton shed is to the right, built by the Midland Railway in 1882. It was a dead end shed with five roads, turntable and coal stage. A one track round house nearby, built in 1867, was demolished c. 1935 to allow the erection of coal and ash plants. The newer shed was closed by BR on January 1, 1968 and the site cleared. WD 'Austerity' Class 2-8-0 locomotive no. 90617 is passing Normanton shed on July 28, 1966. Emerging from Vulcan Foundry during January 1944, the engine was withdrawn from Normanton shed in June 1967 and broken up at Arnott Young of Parkgate. Photograph by Ben Brooksbank.

Opposite below OAKWORTH

Class 2MT 2-6-2T locomotive no.41325, completed at Derby Works in March 1952, heads a train from Keighley up the Worth Valley branch prior to the introduction of DMUs in June 1960. Opened on April 15, 1867 by the Keighley & Worth Valley Railway, the branch line was taken over by the Midland Railway in 1881, then the LMS in 1923. Closure by BR occurred in 1962 but after a long struggle was reopened by the Keighley & Worth Valley Railway Preservation Society in 1968. Photograph from the David Joy collection.

Above PECKFIELD COLLIERY

Once owned by Joseph Cliff & Sons, Peckfield colliery was in production by the 1870s. The colliery's sidings were half a mile west of Micklefield station on the south side of the BR (ex-LNER) line. Closure of the colliery occurred in December 1980 and the Coal Preparation Plant in October 1986. Built by Hunslet in 1952, works no. 3715, 0-6-0ST, *Primrose no. 2*, was moved to Yorkshire Dales Railway, Embsay in December 1973. Photograph taken on May 8, 1972 by Geoff Warnes.

Opposite top OXENHOPE STATION

Originally it was intended that Haworth would be the terminus on the Keighley & Worth Valley but due to pressure it became Oxenhope station which opened with the line on April 15, 1867. As with the rest of the route, it was closed on January 1, 1962, but reopened when the line was preserved in 1968. Oxenhope station presently houses an exhibition shed, where some of the locomotives that are not in use on the line are stored. There is also a station shop, buffet and a car park, and links with local bus services to Bradford and Hebden Bridge. Ivatt Class 4MT 2-6-0 locomotive no. 43114 is pictured at Oxenhope about 1959. Photograph by W. Hubert Foster.

Opposite below ORGREAVES COLLIERY

The signal box on the right was named Orgreaves Colliery; the 's' being added in error and was never changed. Class K3 2-6-0 locomotive no. 61824 is heading northwards, passing the Orgreave colliery railway branch to the left, on April 16, 1955. Photograph by Geoff Warnes.

Above RICCALL

The Selby Diversion was built as a new section of the East Coast Main Line (ECML) to avoid an area of potential subsidence over the Selby Coalfield. Opening in 1983, the line runs roughly northwards from a junction on the ECML, south of Selby, to a junction near Church Fenton, south of York. The new route missed out Riccall and the section of track seen here no longer exists. Raven-designed Class B16 4-6-0 locomotive no 61419, erected at Darlington Works in November, 1920, was withdrawn from York (North) in September 1961. During the following month, it was cut up at Darlington Works. Photograph by Bill Reed.

Opposite top PRINCE OF WALES COLLIERY

Hudswell Clarke built 0-6-0T locomotive no. S.120, works no. 1886, in 1956 but it did not arrive at the Prince of Wales colliery until around 1958. The livery was maroon and black, with yellow lettering on the tank sides. The engine was scrapped on site in December 1972. Prince of Wales colliery closed in December 1980, though colliers were transferred to a drift mine of the same name opened earlier in that year. The surface standard-gauge railway and screens were taken out of use around July 1979. Closure of the drift mine in 2002 brought mining to an end in the area, stretching back nearly 150 years. Photographed by Bill Reed on August 23, 1971.

Opposite below OTTERINGTON STATION

The Great North of England Railway opened Otterington station on March 31, 1841. Rebuilding occurred under the LNER in 1932 and this work included the addition of two new tracks. Although the station closed to passengers on September 15, 1958 and completely on August 10, 1964, the station building, weigh office, loading dock and signal box have been preserved. Peppercorn A1 Class 4-6-2 locomotive no. 60145 *Saint Mungo* dashes through Otterington with 'The Flying Scotsman' service in 1953. Photograph courtesy of *Yorkshire Post Newspapers*.

Above ROBIN HOOD'S BAY STATION

Class A8 4-6-2T locomotive no. 69880 is ready to leave Robin Hood's Bay station *en route* for Whitby on August 3, 1953. Entering service from Darlington Works in June 1921, the engine was rebuilt from Class H1 (4-4-4T) to A8 in 1934 and withdrawn in July 1960. Robin Hood's Bay station was opened by the Scarborough & Whitby Railway on July 16, 1885 and closed completely, March 8, 1965. Photograph by Geoffrey Oates.

Opposite QUEENSBURY STATION

Queensbury station, opened by the Great Northern Railway on April 14 1879, was quite remarkable having platforms on three sides of a triangular junction. The Bradford-Halifax, and Bradford – Keighley lines diverged there and a third side of the triangle was provided by the direct line between Halifax and Keighley. Due to the hilly terrain around Queenbury, the station was built 400ft lower than the village which was 1,150ft above sea level. In the station there were six independent sets of railway offices. Closure to passengers was implemented on May 23, 1955 and to all traffic on November 11 1963. The top picture shows Class J50 0-6-0T locomotive no. 68959 working near Queensbury's north junction. Below, a Class N1 0-6-2T locomotive is seen near the east junction on a Keighley-Bradford Exchange train just before closure in 1955. Both photographs reproduced courtesy of Nigel Callaghan.

Above ROSSINGTON

Rossington station, in the distance, was opened by the Great Northern Railway on September 4, 1849 and closed, October 6 1958. Over the ensuing years much of the site has been cleared. Class A4 4-6-2 locomotive no. 60006 *Sir Ralph Wedgwood* is heading south on August 2, 1952. Entering service from Doncaster Works in January 1938 as *Herring Gull*, this name was removed on December 1, 1943 and replaced with *Sir Ralph Wedgwood* on January 6, 1944. Following an allocation to Aberdeen Ferryhill in May 1964, the engine was withdrawn from there in September 1965. In the following month it was sold for scrap to Motherwell Machinery & Scrap, of Wishaw. Photograph by Geoff Warnes.

Above ROTHERHAM MASBOROUGH

The North Midland Railway opened Rotherham Masborough station, designed by Francis Thompson, on May 11, 1840. It was on the North Midland's route between Derby's tri-junction station and Leeds. Initially, Rotherham Masborough comprised two short staggered platforms and the main station buildings were on the 'Up' side. During the early 20th century, the platforms were extended and spanned by a footbridge. Further alterations took place in the 1920s. Seen in a view looking north east on August 23, 1963 are: 'Black Five' Class 4-6-0 locomotive no. 44871 and Class 46 1Co-Co1 no. D157 on the 'Up' 'Waverley' – Edinburgh via Carlisle – London St Pancras. Photograph by Ben Brooksbank.

Opposite below ROTHERHAM MASBOROUGH

Working in a siding on the west side of Rotherham Masborough station is Johnson Class 1F 0-6-0T locomotive no. 41835. The Vulcan Foundry-built locomotive spent an incredible 74 years and two months in service before withdrawal from Langwith Junction in December 1966. Photographed on May 19, 1956. by Geoff Warnes.

ROTHERHAM MASBOROUGH

Standard Class 9F 2-10-0 locomotive no. 92137 and Class 45 1Co-Co1 locomotive no. D108 are depicted at Rotherham Masborough station in a view facing north west on July 23, 1966. Rotherham Masborough closed on October 3, 1988. Photograph by Geoff Warnes.

Above ROTHERHAM WESTGATE STATION

Stanier Class 3P 2-6-2T locomotive no. 40082 is ready to leave Rotherham Westgate station with a Manchester stopping train on May 17, 1952. The station opened on November 1, 1838 and closed October 6, 1952. Photograph by Geoffrey Oates.

Below ROTHERHAM MASBOROUGH

WD 'Austerity' Class 8 2-8-0 locomotive no. 90156, with fireman posing, is just south of Rotherham Masborough station on September 5, 1964. Photograph by Richard Postill.

Above ROYSTON

It is tempting to suggest 'Black Five' Class 4-6-0 locomotive no. 44822 is waiting at Royston for its driver who is probably about to start a shift on September 15, 1967. The locomotive was withdrawn a month later after almost 23 years in service. Photograph by Geoff Warnes.

Opposite top ROYSTON & NOTTON STATION

In a view looking north, a freight train is rattling through Royston & Notton station, on the ex-Midland Railway main line, with 'Crab' Class 2-6-0 locomotive no. 42794 at the front. Across to the right is Class 4F 0-6-0 locomotive no. 44374 with a 'Down' freight train. Photograph taken on July 24, 1951 by Ben Brooksbank.

Opposite below ROYSTON & NOTTON STATION

Passing Royston & Notton station, on the ex-Midland Railway main line, the 'Up' 'Thames-Clyde Express' (09.20 Glasgow St Enoch to London St Pancras) is double-headed by 'Black Five' Class 4-6-0 locomotive no. 44756 and Jubilee Class 4-6-0 locomotive no. 45615 *Malay States*. Opening on April 6, 1841, the station was resited a mile further south, July 1, 1900, and closed January 1, 1968. Facing north, in the distance, to the right, is Monkton Colliery. Photograph taken on July 24, 1951 by Ben Brooksbank.

Above SAVILE COLLIERY, MICKLETOWN, NEAR METHLEY

Formerly owned by H. Briggs Collieries, Savile colliery opened around 1876 and was connected to the rail network via a line which ran east from BR metals north of Methley station. Lines also ran to a staith on the Aire & Calder navigation to the north of the colliery, and a tip to the east. Around 1965, rail traffic ceased to and from BR, and internal traffic followed in 1982. Savile closed in August 1985. 0-6-0ST *Airedale no. 2* was built by Hunslet in 1939, works no. 1956. Before transferral to Savile in 1962, the engine had spells at Airedale Collieries ltd, Fryston Colliery and Wheldale Colliery. It was scrapped by Wakefield Metal Traders Ltd in November 1975. Photograph taken on September 16, 1971 by Bill Reed.

Opposite top SCARBOROUGH LONDESBOROUGH ROAD STATION

Gresley Class D49 4-4-0 locomotive no. 62739 *The Badsworth* was pictured at Scarborough Londesborough Road station by Bill Reed. Originally the station was named Washbeck Excursion station and opened on June 8, 1908 to relieve the pressure brought on Scarborough station during holiday periods. It was built on the site of an old engine shed and consisted of a 300-yard long through platform and one 250-yard long bay platform. Washbeck became a public station on June 1, 1933 and renamed Scarborough Londesborough Road station; Scarborough station was renamed Scarborough Central. Londesborough closed on August 24, 1963 when excursion services were transferred to Scarborough Central station. The site was subsequently used for storing excursion coaching stock and final closure came in July 1966. Afterwards, the site was redeveloped. Built at Darlington Works, no. 62739 entered service in May 1932 and was withdrawn from Scarborough shed during October 1960.

Opposite below SCARBOROUGH LONDESBOROUGH ROAD STATION

Class K3 2-6-0 locomotive no. 61811 has paused at Scarborough Londesborough Road station in August 1960. Photograph courtesy of Colourrail.

Below SEAMER JUNCTION

Seamer junction is where the Pickering & Seamer (Forge Valley), York – Scarborough and Hull – Scarborough lines once converged. The latter two are still extant but the Forge Valley line was closed from June 5, 1950; the stretch between Thornton Dale and Pickering stayed open until August 10, 1964 to the serve the stone quarry. Class K3 2-6-0 locomotive no. 61853 is passing Seamer Junction on August 25, 1962. Withdrawn from Ardsley during December 1962, no. 61853 had spent nearly 38 years in service. Photograph by Richard Postill.

Above SCARBOROUGH SHED

The York & North Midland Railway opened a two track through shed at Scarborough on July 7, 1845 but it was closed by the NER in 1882 and used as a store. The area was cleared in 1906 for the construction of Londesborough Road excursion station. A second shed, built c.1882 with capacity for 13 engines, included a 44 foot 8 inch turntable. The building was used for engine repairs and storage once the third shed opened 1890. This latter was a brick-built, eight track, dead-ended shed, and could stable 24 engines. It cost £10,000 and included a turntable and water tank. Although officially closing on July 20 1963, the shed was utilized for a time by visiting locomotives until the end of steam. Visible in the picture are: 'Hunt' Class 4-4-0 locomotive no. 62754 *The Berkeley*; and Class B1 locomotive 4-6-0 no. 61112. Photograph courtesy of Kerry Parker.

SELBY SHED

The Leeds & Selby Railway opened Selby's first shed, dead-ended with two tracks, in 1834. It existed until around 1871 and then found use as part of a goods shed. In the same year a second shed was built by the NER south of the station. This facility was a square roundhouse with a slated, triple-hipped roof. In 1898 a new shed of the same design but with a slated triple-gable roof opened adjacent. Facilities available included, a ramped coal stage and water tank. Closure by BR was implemented on September 13, 1959 and the site was later cleared. The two locomotives depicted are: Raven-designed Class B16 4-6-0 no. 61456 and Q6 Class 0-8-0 no. 63448. No. 61456 was allocated to Selby from June 8, 1958 to June 14, 1959. Photograph by Bill Reed.

Above SELBY STATION

The original Selby station was opened by the Leeds & Selby Railway on September 22 1834. It was replaced by a new station built to the north, opening on July 2, 1840. The older station was then converted to goods use and is still extant. The new station was situated on a section of the ECML until the latter was diverted in 1983 to avoid an area of potential subsidence over the Selby Coalfield. The view here, looking north shows, in the distance, Selby swing bridge, dating from 1891 and which replaced a bascule bridge. To the left is the Selby North Box which controlled traffic on the lines over the bridge. The signal box on the bridge gantry controlled the river traffic, which had priority. The 'Up' freight is led by Darlington Works-built Class V2 2-6-2 locomotive no. 60853. Photograph by Rev. J. David Benson and reproduced courtesy of the A1 Steam Locomotive Trust.

Above SETTLE JUNCTION

Pictured at Settle junction, Stanier Class 8F 2-8-0 locomotive no. 48758 is heading a train of empty gypsum wagons on the Settle – Carlisle line to mines near Kirkby Stephen. Built at Doncaster Works, no. 48758 entered service in December 1945. It was first allocated to Crewe, moving to Willesden, Carlisle Canal, Carlisle Kingmoor and finally Newton, being withdrawn from there in June 1964. Photograph taken on September 22, 1962 by Ben Brooksbank.

Opposite top SELBY SHED

Raven Class Q6 0-8-0 locomotive no. 63436 entered traffic from Armstrong Whitworth in June 1922, and was first allocated Borough Gardens. The Q6 engines were occasionally used for medium and long distance freight duties as well as heavy mineral traffic. No. 63436 was allocated to Selby twice during its working life: October 5, 1947 to January 25, 1953 and June 16, 1957 to December 6, 1959. Withdrawal from Sunderland occurred in April 1967 and it was sold as scrap to Hughes Bolckow, of Blyth three months later. Photograph by Bill Reed.

Opposite below SELBY SHED

The B16s were initially described as 'fast goods' locomotives but later they were perhaps more appropriately known for 'mixed traffic' duties. A total of 70 B16s were built at Darlington Works. Class B16 4-6-0 locomotive no. 61433, completed at Darlington in June 1921, was allocated to Selby between September 23, 1956 and June 14, 1959. Withdrawal from York was implemented on November 30, 1959 and the engine retuned to Darlington for scrapping in January 1960. Photograph by Bill Reed.

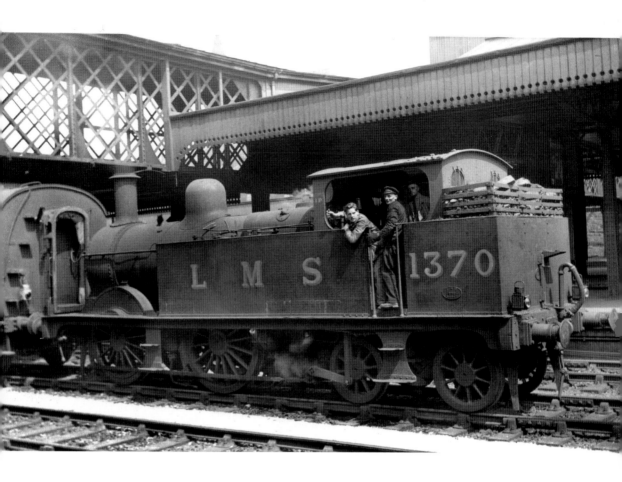

Above SHEFFIELD MIDLAND STATION

Johnson Class 1P-D 0-4-4T locomotive no. 1370 was pictured at Sheffield Midland on July 21, 1951 by Geoffrey Oates. Built by Dubs & Co and entering service in February 1892, the engine was withdrawn from Sheffield Millhouses in February 1953.

Opposite SESSAY STATION

Class V2 2-6-2 locomotive no. 60974 speeds through Sessay station with a Colchester – Newcastle train during the 1950s. The Great North of England line between York and Darlington was opened in March 1841 and Sessay station was providing services by August of the same year. During WWII Sessay station was completely rebuilt, with a platform in the 'Down' direction only, on the new Goods line, but with an island created on the 'Up' side. Closure came on September 15, 1958. Built at Darlington Works, no. 60974 entered traffic in August 1943 at York staying there until withdrawal in December 1963, moving to Darlington for scrapping in January 1964. Photograph courtesy of *Yorkshire Post Newspapers*.

Above SHEFFIELD VICTORIA STATION

Sheffield's second station, Bridgehouses, was a terminus on the new Manchester-Sheffield railway line, and it was opened by the Sheffield, Ashton-under-Lyne & Manchester Railway (SA&M) on July 14, 1845. In time, Bridgehouses' facilities became inadequate, so in the late 1840s work started on an extension and a new station – Victoria – built by the Manchester Sheffield & Lincoln Railway (superseding the SA&M in 1846) to the east. Bridghouses subsequently closed to passenger traffic and became the MS&L's terminal for goods, mineral and cattle traffic, with very large and convenient warehouses and coal drops. John Fowler, who later co-designed Scotland's Forth Railway Bridge, was responsible for the extension and Victoria station. Included was a 40-foot high, 600 yard viaduct over the Wicker. Sheffield Victoria station and the Woodhead route linking Sheffield and Manchester closed on January 5, 1970. Services were transferred to the Hope Valley line. Class D11/1 4-4-0 locomotive no. 62669 *Ypres* was pictured at Sheffield Victoria on September 6, 1958 by Geoff Warnes.

Opposite top SHEFFIELD MIDLAND STATION

Opened by the Midland Railway on February 1, 1870, the station was initially known as Sheffield New Midland; Sheffield Midland, February 1, 1876; Sheffield City, September 25, 1950; and Sheffield, following the closure of Sheffield Victoria in January 1970. Enlarged and remodelled in 1904-5, to the designs of the Midland's architect Charles Trubshaw, the station underwent further alterations in 1956-7 when the original train shed was removed and replaced by platform extensions with canopies. Further remodelling occurred in 2002 and included the construction of a new footbridge, station approach and public square. Class B1 4-6-0 locomotive no. 61092 was photographed by Bill Wright on September 18, 1965.

Opposite below SHEFFIELD MIDLAND STATION

Class 2MT 2-6-0 locomotive no. 46402 waits to depart from Sheffield Midland station with the 09.39 all stations train to Chinley on February 28, 1966. Built at Crewe Works, the engine entered traffic in December 1946 and was withdrawn from Buxton in June 1967. Scrapping followed in January 1968. Photograph by Bill Wright.

Above SHEFFIELD VICTORIA STATION

Victoria station was covered by a ridge and furrow roof of iron and glass measuring 83 feet by 400 feet and constructed by Fox, Henderson, and Co. The arches on which the station rested were built by Miller, Blackie and Shortridge. Improvements were made in 1867 and 1875 respectively and towards the end of the 19th century further plans were mooted. It was hoped these would satisfy the complaints from the public over the inadequacy of the existing accommodation. One of the suggestions was to improve the approach to the station. Director Class 4-4-0 locomotive no. 62661 *Gerard Powys Dewhurst*, completed at Gorton Works in February 1920, was allocated to Sheffield Darnall from June 14, 1958 to June 13, 1959 and on the latter day it was photographed by Geoff Warnes.

Opposite top SHEFFIELD VICTORIA STATION

Under British Railways, in the post war years, Victoria enjoyed a boom. Express services from Manchester London Road ran via the station on the old Great Central line to London Marylebone, others travelled on the East Coast Main Line to London King's Cross. The trains included the 'Master Cutler', 'Sheffield Pullman' and 'South Yorkshireman'. Class B17 4-6-0 locomotive no. 61620 *Clumber* was photographed by Geoff Warnes on September 6, 1958. Built at Darlington Works, the engine went into service during November 1930 and during its working life was allocated to Cambridge, March and King's Lynn sheds, being withdrawn in January 1960.

Opposite below SHEFFIELD VICTORIA STATION

Opening a new ladies waiting room and general waiting room at Victoria on 23 July 1957, the deputy Sheffield Lord Mayor, Ald. R. Neil said: 'I never thought I should see anything like this on a railway station'. This was all part of a station refurbishment and modernisation scheme. Sadly, Victoria's post war traffic boom and fresh appearance did not last very long. The station's last train, an enthusiast's special, arrived at 00.44 on January 5 1970 and thereafter it was shut. Class K2 2-6-0 locomotive no. 61778 eases into Sheffield Victoria on September 6, 1958. Photograph by Geoff Warnes.

Above SHEFFIELD MIDLAND STATION

Looking north, with Sheffield's controversial Park Hill flats complex on the right, three locomotives are featured here at the Midland station. They are: Jubilee Class 4-6-0 no. 45683 *Hogue*; Class K3 2-6-0 no. 61864; and 'Crab' Class 2-6-0 no. 42768. Photograph taken on August 4, 1962 by Geoff Warnes.

Opposite top SHEFFIELD MIDLAND STATION

The Midland Railway's proposal for a new Sheffield station caused controversy from the outset. The Duke of Norfolk, who owned land in the area, insisted that the southern approach be in a tunnel and the land known as The Farm landscaped to prevent the line being visible. Sheffield Town Council insisted that public access be maintained across the station as it was feared the eastern part of the town would be cut off from the rest of Sheffield. In a view facing north, Jubilee Class 4-6-0 locomotive no. 45694 *Bellerophon* eases out of Sheffield Midland on August 4, 1962. Bellerophon was a hero of Greek mythology. Entering service from Crewe Works in March 1936, the engine was withdrawn from Wakefield in January 1967. Photographed by Geoff Warnes.

Opposite below SHEFFIELD VICTORIA STATION

On April 9, 1966 Class B1 4-6-0 locomotive no. 61137 is working the 19.50 train to Swindon from Sheffield Victoria. There was a brief flicker of life back at Victoria on January 7, 1973 when trains were diverted whilst Sheffield Midland was temporarily closed for re-signalling. With the exception of a single track goods avoiding line, still existing to serve the Stocksbridge steelworks, all the station's track was lifted in the mid-1980s. On August 11, 1986 the *Sheffield Star* reported, Victoria station, which had stood idle for years, was all but demolished: 'The 400-foot by 80 foot glass canopy of a roof was an iron skeleton, the handsome Greenmoor stone buildings were crashing to the ground under the demolition hammer'. Photograph by Geoff Warnes.

Above SHIPLEY

Compound Class 4-4-0 locomotive no. 41067, completed at Derby Works in August 1924, approaches Shipley station. These locomotives were once the standard motive power on expresses such as the 'Morecambe Residential', completing the journey from Leeds in well under two hours. The Midland signal-box on the left controlled the junction with the Ilkley branch, while on right is the Great Northern box that until 1968 handled freight traffic on the line climbing to Idle and Laisterdyke. Shipley station was opened on July 16, 1846 and resited to the north in the summer of 1849. No. 41067 was withdrawn from Manningham in February 1955. Photograph from the David Joy collection.

Opposite top SKIPTON STATION

Skipton station was opened on September 8, 1847 by the Leeds & Bradford Extension Railway at a cost of approx. £2,300. By 1851 the company had been absorbed by the Midland Railway who moved the station further north on April 30, 1876. Comprising four platforms, the station cost over £15,000. The opening of the new station coincided with the Midland beginning services on their Settle – Carlisle Line. Thus, Skipton was now on the London St Pancras to Glasgow main line. Further platforms were added in October 1888. Class 4P locomotive no. 42491 is departing Skipton on April 18, 1960. Entering service from Derby Works in April 1937 the engine was allocated to Newton Heath, then moved to Hellifield and Speke junction before withdrawal in September 1963. Scrapping was carried out during March 1964. Photograph by Geoff Warnes.

Opposite below SKIPTON STATION

'Crab' Class 2-6-0 locomotive no. 42810 stands at Skipton on April 18, 1960. Photograph by Geoff Warnes.

Below SLEDMERE & FIMBER STATION

During September 1957, Worsdell Class J27 0-6-0 locomotive no. 65849 is in charge of a weekly 10.10am Malton to Selby pick-up freight train at Sledmere & Fimber station. Photograph reproduced courtesy of A.M. Ross.

Above SLEDMERE & FIMBER STATION

The station was opened as Fimber on June 1, 1853 by the Malton & Driffield Junction Railway. It was renamed Sledmere in 1858 and Sledmere & Fimber a year later. In 1876 a small lockup warehouse for parcels was provided. Serving the Sykes' Sledmere estate, the station was provided with a private waiting room for Sir Taton Sykes but was converted to a 'first class' waiting room in 1860. Thirty years later the room became a ladies waiting room when the station was renovated during the 1890s. The alterations included the platform being raised and lengthened leaving a small section of the original low platform in front of the main station building. Queen Victoria used the station in the 1880s and on July 6, 1948 King George VI and Queen Elizabeth travelled by train to the station when they stayed at Sledmere House. Sledmere & Fimber closed to passengers on June 5, 1950 and completely October 2, 1958. Pictured at the station on September 25, 1958 are: stationmaster, Charles Russell (in peaked cap), porter/signalman, Alan Birdsall (left); a train guard, fireman and driver. They are with Class J39 0-6-0 locomotive no. 64928 which was allocated to Malton between October 26, 1952 and July 21, 1961. Withdrawal occurred on the latter date. Photograph reproduced courtesy of A.M. Ross.

Above SOWERBY BRIDGE STATION

A spectacular panoramic view of Sowerby Bridge station illustrates Jubilee Class 4-6 0 locomotive no. 45717 *Dauntless* heading a Liverpool – York express train made up entirely of carriages in 'plum and spilt milk' livery. The station was opened on October 5, 1840 by the Manchester & Leeds Railway but was resited further east by the L&Y on September 1, 1876. This latter station was severely damaged by fire in October 1978 and subsequently demolished by British Rail in 1980. A replacement station was built in 1981 but it is now unstaffed. Photograph by Eric Treacy.

Opposite top SOUTH KIRKBY COLLIERY

South Kirkby colliery was completed in two phases. The Ferryhill & Rosedale Iron Company reached the Barnsley seam in August, 1878 but their finances ran out. A new limited company, with John Shaw, of Darrington Hall, as chairman, took over in 1880 and the work on South Kirkby colliery was concluded. Under the NCB, there were two connections to the British Rail network: one north-west of South Elmsall station; and another at the southern end of the colliery area. The colliery ceased using surface locomotives around September 1970 and closed itself in March 1988. NCB no. 1 *John Shaw*, presumably named after the former colliery chairman, entered service from Hunslet in 1942. The engine was scrapped on site by Thos W. Ward Ltd, Sheffield, in January 1972. To the rear is 0-4-0ST *York no. 1*. Photographed by Bill Reed on April 5, 1971.

Opposite below SPROTBROUGH

Built at Doncaster Works Class 4MT 2-6-0 locomotive no. 43159, is running light engine with another locomotive (unidentified) through Sprotbrough on the Doncaster Avoiding Line. The line opened for goods and mineral traffic on July 25, 1910 and for passenger traffic four days later. Photograph taken by George Firth.

Above STAINFORTH, NORTH YORKSHIRE

On the former Midland Railway's Settle – Carlisle line, Class 4P 2-6-4T locomotive no. 42472 heads a Garsdale to Hellifield local service past Stainforth sidings in July 1961. One of the most scenic and impressive railways in the UK, the Settle – Carlisle line was opened for freight traffic in August 1875 and passenger travel in 1876, having taken six years to construct. It comprises 72 miles of track with 21 viaducts spanning the ravines and 14 tunnels. Much of the line, from Carlisle to Dent, is in Cumbria, with the section between Ribblehead and Settle in North Yorkshire. No. 42472 was one of 206 in the class, building work being carried out by Derby Works (133) and NBLC (73). Completed at Derby Works in December 1936, no 42472 was withdrawn from Gorton in November 1962 and broken up at Cashmore's during October 1963. Photograph by Derek Cross.

Opposite top STAINFORTH, NORTH YORKSHIRE

The cost of the Settle – Carlisle line was £3.6 million (equivalent to £300 million in 2016) 50 per cent above the estimate and a colossal sum for the time. The line was part of the Midland Railway's London – Glasgow route and for a time the entire stretch enjoyed a boom period but fell away after Grouping and during nationalisation. This brought to an end several services: 'The Waverley' from London St Pancras to Edinburgh Waverley via Nottingham in 1968; and 'The Thames-Clyde Express' from London to Glasgow St Enoch via Leicester in 1975. Clan Class 4-6-2 locomotive no. 72006 *Clan McKenzie* is on an 'Up' train at Stainforth, North Yorkshire, June 28, 1963. Entering service from Crewe Works in February 1952, the engine – apart from a short stint at Haymarket – was allocated to Carlisle Kingmoor during its working life of just over 14 years. Photograph by Rodney Lissenden.

Opposite below STAINFORTH, NORTH YORKSHIRE

Facing north, Fowler Class 2P 4-4-0 locomotive no. 40685 heads an easy load – a milk tanker and brake van – past Stainforth Sidings, North Yorkshire in June 1958. The circular openings in the wall on the right of the loco are part of the Hoffmann lime kiln, which went into continuous production in 1873 to coincide with the building of the Settle-Carlisle railway. Built at Derby Works and entering service in April 1932, the locomotive was allocated to Hellifield from September 8, 1956 until withdrawal in July 1961. Photograph courtesy of *Yorkshire Post Newspapers*.

Above STAINFORTH LANE, SOUTH YORKSHIRE

WD Class 2-8-0 locomotive no. 90369 is working along Stainforth Lane, Doncaster on March 12, 1966. Built by NBLC, the locomotive entered traffic in October 1944 and was withdrawn from Doncaster in April 1966. Photograph by Geoff Warnes.

Opposite top STAINFORTH, SOUTH YORKSHIRE

From a lofty position at Stainforth Yard on February 12, 1955, photographer Geoff Warnes has caught a unique cab view of J11 0-6-0 locomotive no. 64348. The locomotive driver has a steady hand on the regulator, and the fireman is ready to feed the glowing fire. The engine was withdrawn from Colwick in March 1960 after almost 56 years in service.

Opposite below STAINFORTH YARD, SOUTH YORKSHIRE

The first railway to reach Stainforth was the South Yorkshire Railway extending from Doncaster to Thorne. The single line ran along the southern bank of the River Don and initially terminated at Thorne Waterside station. It opened for freight in December 1855 and passengers in July 1856. One of the main purposes of the new railway was to transport coal from the South Yorkshire area to Thorne from where the mineral could be shipped to Hull and other ports. The station at Stainforth was situated on the East Bank but the railway was abandoned in 1866, superseded by a more direct, straighter line from Doncaster to Thorne opened by the Manchester, Sheffield & Lincolnshire Railway company. A new station at Stainforth was built close to the Stainforth/Hatfield boundary and opened on October 1, 1866. During the 20th century, lines were increased in the area to accommodate workings at the adjacent Hatfield colliery, Stainforth & Keadby Canal and traffic to and from the steel works at Scunthorpe. Quite a gathering of railway staff pose for the camera with Class J11 0-6-0 locomotive no. 64348 at Stainforth Yard on February 12, 1955. Photograph by Geoff Warnes.

Above STAITHES VIADUCT

The Staithes viaduct was built in 1875 but not opened to railway traffic until the North Eastern Railway's Teeside to Whitby via the coast line was completed on December 3, 1883. Built of iron and concrete, the viaduct had a speed restriction of 20 mph for trains travelling across in high winds. The structure was fitted with wheel guards so trains would not be swept away during strong gusts and measuring equipment set to ring a bell in a signal box when wind reached a dangerous level. Staithes viaduct is seen here looking north west with an unidentified locomotive passing along during the 1950s. The viaduct was demolished in 1960. Photograph reproduced courtesy of Neil Cholmondeley.

Opposite top STAITHES STATION

Opening with the line on December 3, 1883 Staithes station comprised a main building (on the 'Down' platform) and a wooden waiting shelter on the 'Up' platform. A signal box at the station's south end controlled traffic into a small goods yard. The station closed completely on May 5, 1958. Track through the station was lifted in the following year. All the station buildings incorporating the stationmaster's house survive as a private residence, but the 'Up' platform has been cleared. Thompson Class L1 2-6-4T locomotive no.67765 has paused on the 'Down' platform during the 1950s. Built at NBLC, the engine was withdrawn from Ardsley during November 1962 after almost 14 years in service. Photograph reproduced courtesy of Neil Cholmondeley.

Opposite below STAITHES STATION

Facing north-west, the view shows Thompson Class L1 2-6-4T locomotive no. 67754 on the 'Up' line during the 1950s. Photograph reproduced courtesy of Neil Cholmondeley.

Above STANLEY STATION

Stanley station was situated on the Methley Joint Railway (MJR), the brainchild of the Great Northern Railway, but the North Eastern and Lancashire & Yorkshire Railway Companies were admitted as partners. The MJR stretched, from a double junction at Lofthouse, five miles eastwards to Methley, where it joined the NER and L&Y lines. The line opened for freight in 1865 and passengers in 1869. Stanley station, the only intermediate one on the MJR, opened on May 1, 1869. Class N1 0-6-2T no. 69471 eases over the gated level crossing, carrying the Wakefield – Aberford Road, while entering Stanley station with a train from Castleford Central to Leeds Central in April 1954. Stanley station closed on November 2, 1964; the line's eastern section was used to Newmarket colliery until 1980. Photograph by H.C. Casserley.

Opposite top STOURTON

On a southbound express out of Leeds, Jubilee Class 4-6-0 locomotive no. 45675 *Hardy* has just passed beneath the iron bridge carrying a line from Beeston junction across to Hunslet East and Neville Hill (all gone now and the bridge removed). To service from Crewe Works in December 1935, no. 45675 was withdrawn from Crewe North in June 1967. Photograph taken on April 22, 1953 and reproduced courtesy of *Yorkshire Post Newspapers*.

Opposite below SWINTON TOWN STATION

Swinton Town station was opened on July 1, 1840; renamed Swinton 1852/3; and resited around 200 yards further north on July 2, 1899. The station had four platform faces on two island platforms, one set between the 'Up' and 'Down' main lines, the other between the 'Up' and 'Down' slow lines. Access to the platforms was by a path and subway from the booking office. Both platforms had wooden waiting rooms. The main station building was at road level and this contained the booking office, parcels office and stationmaster's room. Renamed Swinton Town on September 25, 1958, closure came on January 1, 1968. Stanier Class 8F 2-8-0 locomotive no. 48037 is at the head of a freight train at Swinton Town station. To service from Vulcan Foundry in September 1936, the engine was withdrawn from Toton in December 1965. Photograph from John Law collection.

Above STOURTON

Hurrying south, past Wakefield Road bridge, with a Leeds – Bristol express is 'Black Five' Class 4-6-0 locomotive no. 44853. Entering service from Crewe Works in November 1944, the engine was withdrawn from Holbeck in June 1967. On the left is Wakefield Road signal box. The bridge has since been replaced by a larger concrete structure. Photograph taken on April 22, 1953 and reproduced courtesy of *Yorkshire Post Newspapers*.

Opposite top and below SWINTON, WATH ROAD

Two views taken looking south to Queen Street Bridge on May 28, 1960 show two different locomotives travelling along Wath Road, Swinton to Mexborough West Junction. They are Fowler Class 4F 0-6-0 no. 44071 and Riddles Standard Class 9F 2-10-0 no. 92135. Introduced to traffic from NBLC in November 1925, no 44071 was withdrawn from Staveley (Barrow Hill) in April 1963. No. 92135 was completed at Crewe Works in June 1957 and was withdrawn from Wakefield in June 1967. The line here was a link between Mexborough West Junction and Swinton Junction curve. Both photographs were taken by Geoff Warnes.

THIRSK

Class A2/2 4-6-2 (formerly P2 Class 2-8-2) locomotive no. 60502 *Earl Marischal* is drawing a train four miles south of Thirsk during February 1953. Before withdrawal from York in July 1961, the engine had spent just under 26 years 9 months in service. Photograph reproduced courtesy of *Yorkshire Post Newspapers*.

Above THORNE JUNCTION

'Black Five' Class locomotive no. 44841, working a Chesterfield and Sheffield excursion to Cleethorpes on June 25, 1961, is fast approaching Thorne junction. Over to the right is Hatfield Main colliery (closed 2015). A new double line railway from Doncaster which splits two ways at Thorne Junction was opened in two stages by the MS&L in 1866 and 1869. One of the main aims was to move coal more easily by rail to the ports. The first line ran eastwards to meet a link to Scunthorpe and Grimsby; the second one ran north to connect to a North Eastern line with Goole and Hull. Thorne South railway station opened on the first line on September 10, 1866; Thorne North on the second one August 2, 1869. Built at Crewe Works in October 1944, no. 44841 was withdrawn from Oxley in October 1966. Photograph by Geoff Warnes.

Above THORNHILL
An unidentified Class 8F 2-8-0 locomotive working a freight train is depicted at Thornhill on April 19, 1962.
Photograph by Geoff Warnes.

Opposite top THORNE JUNCTION
Class O4 2-8-0 locomotive no. 63793 is light engine at Kirton Lane bridge, Thorne on June 25, 1961. Initially there was a level crossing here instead of a bridge. Completed at NBLC, in February 1918, no. 63793 remained in service until withdrawal from Froddingham in May 1965. Photograph by Geoff Warnes.

Opposite below THORNE JUNCTION
After leaving the Scunthorpe/Grimsby line, Class O4 2-8-0 locomotive no. 63652 has just passed Thorne Junction box on June 25, 1961 whilst heading west with a train of empties. The line to the left heads to Thorne North, and onwards to Goole and Hull. Built by Kitson and entering traffic in March 1918, the engine was later classified as O4/4 and O1 and withdrawn from Staveley during November 1963. Photograph from Kirton Lane Bridge by Geoff Warnes.

Above TICKHILL

To oversee the construction of a new railway in South Yorkshire, a committee was formed under the title of South Yorkshire Joint Railway and included the Great Central Railway, the Great Northern Railway, the Lancashire & Yorkshire Railway, the Midland Railway and the North Eastern Railway. Each company had equal rights over the predominantly single line and it extended from Dinnington to Kirk Sandal. It opened to freight on January 1, 1909 and passengers on December 1, 1910. The SYJR was 21.25 miles (34km) in length, including its colliery branch lines and connections to the several lines it crossed in its path. There were three stations on the railway which also served a number of collieries. Passenger services ceased in 1929 and all the collieries have since closed. Class WD 'Austerity' 2-8-0 locomotive no. 90704 is heading a train through Tickhill on the South Yorkshire Joint Railway on August 8, 1953. Built at Vulcan Foundry and entering service in February 1945, the engine had allocations at Hull Dairycoates, Hull Springhead and Goole before withdrawal in June 1967. Picture by Geoff Warnes.

Opposite top THURNSCOE SIDINGS

WD 'Austerity' 2-8-0 Class locomotive no. 90654 is working at Thurnscoe Dearne Valley Railway sidings on March 4, 1966. Once a small farming village Thurnscoe was extensively developed to accommodate miners at the nearby Hickleton colliery which closed in October 1991. From BR lines, sidings ran east to Hickleton colliery and adjacent brickworks. Building of the 2-8-0, R.A. Riddles-designed class was divided between the NBLC and Vulcan Foundry. Once ubiquitous throughout the railway system, especially in colliery areas like South Yorkshire, only one WD has survived into preservation. Vulcan Foundry works no. 5200 was repatriated from Sweden to the Keighley & Worth Valley Railway in 1973. Vulcan Foundry-built no. 90654 entered service in August 1944 and was withdrawn during June 1967. Photograph by Geoff Warnes.

Opposite below THORPE MARSH

Vulcan Foundry-built Class B1 4-6-0 locomotive no. 61189 is rushing through Thorpe Marsh on July 17, 1960 with a Blackpool – Cleethorpes excursion train. At this time the engine was allocated to Copley Hill, Leeds (February 22, 1959 to August 20, 1961). Photograph by Geoff Warnes.

Above TICKHILL & WADWORTH STATION

Robinson Class O4 2-8-0 locomotive no. 63585 has paused at Tickhill station on the SYJ line with a 'Gainsborough Model Railway Society Special' train. Tickhill station first opened with a Sunday School excursion to Cleethorpes on July 6, 1910. The public opening occurred on December 1, 1910. The station became Tickhill & Wadworth on July 1, 1911; closed in April 1926, reopened on July 25, 1927; and closed on July 8, 1929. The site has been cleared. No. 63585 was withdrawn from Retford in December 1963 after just over 52 years in service. Photograph by George Firth.

Opposite top WAKEFIELD SHED

There have been four locomotive sheds in Wakefield and the one relevant to this picture was opened in 1893. Erected by the L&Y in brick, it was a 10 track dead-ended shed including a coal stage with water tank over and a turntable. In time the shed was converted to a 10-track through shed with a new coaling plant and turntable added in 1932. Further alterations were made in 1956 and closure came on June 3, 1967. Demolition occurred in 1993. Built by the NBLC and entering traffic in January 1947, Class B1 4-6-0 locomotive no. 61115 was allocated to Wakefield on November 13, 1966. Withdrawal was affected from there on May 8, 1967. Photograph by Bill Reed.

Opposite below WAKEFIELD KIRKGATE STATION

Class V2 2-6-2 locomotive no 60876 heads through Wakefield Kirkgate station with a through freight train on July, 22 1965. Built at Doncaster Works in May 1940, the engine was withdrawn from York in October 1965. Wakefield Kirkgate was opened on October 5, 1840. Over the years it has also been known as Wakefield Junction and Wakefield Kirkgate Joint. The station's overall roof and some platform buildings were removed in 1972 before Kirkgate was listed with Grade II status. After many years of neglect, a major scheme to restore the station commenced in August 2013. This £4.6 million project was driven by Groundwork Wakefield and multiple funding partners and will hopefully see the facilities brought back to life. Photograph by Bill Wright.

WAKEFIELD KIRKGATE STATION

WD 'Austerity' Class 2-8-0 locomotive no. 90112 is light engine at Wakefield Kirkgate station on July 22, 1965. Built at NBLC in March 1943, no. 90112 was allocated to Wakefield between June 14, 1958 and December 3, 1966. Withdrawal from Sunderland occurred in January 1967. Photograph by Bill Wright.

Above WAKEFIELD WESTGATE STATION

The original Wakefield Westgate station opened on October 5, 1857 but was moved just 10 chains north from May 1, 1867. It was built for the Great Northern, Midland and Manchester, Sheffield & Lincolnshire Railways. Ivatt Class 4 2-6-0 locomotive no. 43043 eases through the station on a down freight on June 6, 1967. Photograph by Bill Wright.

Below WAKEFIELD SHED

Featured here at Wakefield shed on October 30, 1966 are: 'Black Five' Class 4-6-0 locomotive no. 44944; Jubilee Class locomotive no 4-6-0 no. 45739 *Ulster*; Class B1 locomotive 4-6-0 no. 61173. Photograph by Bill Wright.

Above WATH YARD

Wath Yard was opened in 1907 with the intention of providing a large area for coal traffic from surrounding collieries to be concentrated and then sorted for transportation to many different areas of the country. Construction work on the yard was carried out by Logan & Hemingway. It was built on the 'hump' idea, where trains of wagons were uncoupled and then individually propelled over a hump, allowing them to run by gravity into their allotted sidings to await transportation. But, unlike later hump yards, it did not have automatic retarders to slow down the rolling wagons. To do this job, men were employed to 'chase' wagons and 'pin down' their brakes. Steam locomotives used in the yard were supplied by Mexborough shed but following their demise around 1963 a two road facility for the electric locomotives used was erected. The late 20th century saw a rapid decline in the use of coal as energy, resulting in the yard closing in 1988. Class S1 0-8-4T locomotive no. 69904, seen here on May 2, 1953, was one of six built especially for work in Wath Yard. The first batch of four locomotives built by Beyer Peacock Ltd appeared in 1907. The second group was erected at Gorton Works in 1932; no. 69904 belongs to this latter batch. Photograph by Geoff Warnes.

Opposite top WARMSWORTH, A1 MOTORWAY

On April 9, 1960, Class O2 2-8-0 locomotive no. 63935 passes construction work taking place for a bridge to carry the A1 motorway across the Warmsworth cutting. Entering traffic from Doncaster Works in November 1923, the engine was first allocated to New England. Withdrawal from Grantham occurred in September 1963 and in February 1964, no. 63935 was broken up at Rigleys, Bulwell Forest. Photograph by Geoff Warnes.

Opposite below WARMSWORTH CUTTING

The South Yorkshire Railway's line from Swinton to Doncaster involved cutting through solid limestone rock at Warmsworth. A ceremonial first sod was cut at Warmsworth in October 1847 and the line opened in July 1849. The picture below taken by Geoff Warnes on May 10, 1959, looking west, shows both a section of the cutting and an unidentified Class O2 2-8-0 locomotive awaiting signals.

Above WHITBY TOWN STATION

Worsdell Class G5 0-4-4T locomotive no. 67240 is pictured at Whitby Town station on August 3, 1953. Completed at Darlington Works during May 1894, the engine was allocated to Whitby between July 25, 1953 and December 17, 1955. Withdrawal was from Malton in April 1956. Photograph by Geoffrey Oates.

Opposite top WHELDALE COLLIERY

Wheldale colliery opened in 1868 and the colliery sidings were on the north side of the York-Normanton (later LNER) line and situated north-east of Castleford Central station. Hunslet's 0-6-0ST *Bawtry* was built in 1932, works no. 1698. In 1947 the locomotive was noted as ex-Airedale Collieries then spent time at Newmarket colliery and Allerton Bywater Central Workshops before returning to Wheldale in March 1967. Photographed by Bill Reed in 1971, the end came for *Bawtry* in December 1972 when it was scrapped on site by W.H. Arnott, Young & Co. Ltd, Bradford. Wheldale colliery closed in 1987.

Opposite below WHELDALE COLLIERY

Built in 1943, Hunslet's 0-6-0ST locomotive, works no. 2879, was ex-Waterloo Main colliery and Allerton Bywater Central Workshops before it moved to Wheldale in September 1970. Photographed by Bill Reed on September 16, 1971, the engine is seen in the fully lined NCB maroon and red livery. From Wheldale the engine moved to Newmarket colliery in October 1973, and from there to Springwell Central Workshops in January 1975. The engine is currently located at the Caledonian Railway (Brechin) Ltd.

Above WHITBY SHED

The York & North Midland Railway opened a one track shed at Whitby with a turntable in June 1847 but it was rebuilt in 1868 to a two track dead-ended facility. There was a 50ft table (enlarged to 60ft in 1936), water column and coal stage at the shed. Closure came on April 6, 1959 and the building has been put to various uses since that time. Riddles Standard Class 4 2-6-4T locomotive no. 80118 entered service from Brighton Works in June 1955 and was allocated new to Whitby. The engine stayed there until June 14, 1958 when subsequent moves were made to Neville Hill, Carstairs and Polmadie where withdrawal occurred in November 1966. Also just visible is Class H1 (later A8) 4-4-4T locomotive no. 69865. Completed at Darlington in March 1918 and allocated to Whitby at the end of May 1948, the engine was withdrawn from there in April 1958. Photograph courtesy of Kerry Parker.

Opposite top WHITBY SHED

An extensive view, looking north east, of Whitby shed with a varied selection of locomotives present in May 1958. The stone-built shed was situated on the west side of the former Whitby & Pickering line and south of the station. Photograph reproduced courtesy of Colourrail.

Opposite below WHITBY TOWN STATION

A station at Whitby was opened by the Whitby & Pickering Railway on June 8, 1835. A new station, designed by G.T. Andrews was opened nearby by the York & North Midland Railway on June 4, 1847. The station was known as Whitby Town 1886 to 1924 and September 30, 1951 to September 5, 1966. The station was Listed Grade II in December 1972. Class D49 4-4-0 locomotive no. 62731 *Selkirkshire* is visible at the station on June 23, 1957. Photograph courtesy of Colourrail.

Above **WHITBY TOWN STATION**

Class V1 2-6-2T locomotive no. 67639 is waiting to depart Whitby Town station on July 31, 1953. Built at Doncaster Works, the engine entered service in June 1935. A total of 82 V1s were built between 1930 and 1939 in five batches. The V1 was a comparatively powerful engine suited to heavy and tightly-timed suburban workings. In the post-War era no. 67639 was allocated to north eastern sheds: Middlesbrough (twice), Heaton Blaydon and Gateshead. Withdrawal was implemented in October 1962. Photograph by Geoffrey Oates.

Opposite **WHITBY WEST CLIFF STATION**

The North Eastern Railway leased the Whitby, Redcar & Middlesbrough Union Railway, extending between Whitby and Loftus, from July 1875. Whitby West Cliff station opened on December 3, 1883. It was designed by NER architect William Bell and on the 'Up' platform was the main brick-built station edifice incorporating the stationmaster's house. A brick-built structure on the 'Down' platform included a waiting area. The station closed on June 12, 1961 and for a period was used as a council depot. Around 2000, the area was redeveloped for an imaginative housing scheme, the overall design incorporating the station buildings. Thompson Class L1 2-6-4T locomotive no. 67764 pulls into the 'Down' platform at Whitby West Cliff in May 1958. To service from the NBLC in February 1949, the engine was withdrawn from Low Moor in August 1962. Photograph courtesy of Colourrail.

WINCOBANK

In a view looking east across to the cooling towers at Tinsley, an unidentified 'Black Five' Class 4-6-0 locomotive is at Wincobank junction, Sheffield, with an express passenger service. Photograph taken on August 1, 1960 by Geoff Warnes.

Above YORK

No. 60102 *Sir Frederick Banbury* was the second of the Gresley A1 Pacifics to be built when completed at Doncaster Works in July 1922. Originally numbered GNR 1471, it was later to carry numbers: 1471N; 4471, 501 (not applied); 102 and eventually 60102, from May 1949. The engine was named on November 10, 1922 and the first allocation was to Doncaster where it initially spent just over 10 years. The engine returned there again twice over its working life. *Sir Frederick Banbury* was rebuilt to A3 in October 1942 and received a double chimney in April 1959. The engine was withdrawn from King's Cross in November 1961 and cut up at Doncaster shortly afterwards. Photograph by Bill Reed.

Above YORK STATION

Standard Class 3 2-6-0 locomotive no. 77004 pauses at York station on August 29, 1963. Completed at Swindon Works in March 1954, the engine was first allocated to Darlington but was based at York North at the time of the picture. Withdrawal from Stourton came in June 1966 and no. 77004 was scrapped at T.W. Ward, Beighton. Photograph by Richard Postill.

Opposite top WORSBROUGH

Ben Brooksbank took this photograph from Strafforth Crossing looking west on April 28, 1950, just before electrification. Peppercorn Class K1 2-6-0 locomotive no, 62015 is at the front of a train of empties descending Worsbrough Bank. Completed at NBLC in July 1949, the engine was allocated to Gorton when new and this lasted until May 21, 1950. Withdrawal from Frodingham was no. 62015's fate in July 1965.

Opposite below YORK STATION

The first station to serve York was a temporary terminus built by the York & North Midland Railway in May 1839. The city's second station was opened in January in January 1841 by the Y&NM and the Great North of England Railway (later NER). The station was in use until its replacement by the present station, which is situated to the west of the second station. It was opened on June 25, 1877 by the NER to a curved pattern with 13 platforms. Class J72 0-6-0T locomotive no. 68735 rests beneath a typical NER signal gantry at York. These installations were familiar sights at this busy junction for many years and a good number of them survived until the introduction of colour light signalling in 1951. Completed by Armstrong Whitworth during 1922, the locomotive was withdrawn from York in October 1958. Photograph taken on April 21, 1951 by Geoffrey Oates.

YORK

Class A3 locomotive no. 60082 *Neil Gow* entered traffic as an A1 from NBLC in November 1924 and was named in November 1925. The first allocation was to Heaton where it returned on three more occasions. Rebuilding to A3 at Doncaster Works was completed in January 1943. Withdrawal from Gateshead occurred in September 1963 and the engine was cut up at Darlington Works. *Neil Gow* was photographed at York North shed by Bill Reed.

Above YORK

An unidentified Class 8F 2-8-0 locomotive is pictured at York North shed alongside Jubilee Class 4-6-0 locomotive no. 45694 *Bellerophon*. Completed at Crewe Works in March 1936, no 45694 was withdrawn from Wakefield in January 1967. Photograph taken on March 19, 1966 by Geoff Warnes.

Below YORK

Worsdell Class J27 0-6-0 locomotive no. 65894 was completed at Darlington Works in September 1923. The engine is located in the yard sidings attached to York North shed adjacent to the railway station. It is perhaps engaged in handling coal wagons going on to the main coal hopper. Visible behind its chimney is the yard turntable. No. 65894 was withdrawn from Sunderland in September 1967. Photograph taken by Bill Reed.

YORK NORTH SHED

York North shed was opened by the North Eastern Railway in 1878 and comprised three sheds, nos 1, 2, and 3. Nos 1 and 2 were subsequently rebuilt and a fourth shed was added in 1959. Amongst the facilities were a coaling plant, water tank and turntable. In April 1943 the shed was bombed during an air raid and a number of locomotives were destroyed. Rebuilding occurred in 1954 with sheds 1 and 2 being demolished and replaced by a seven track through road shed. Sheds 3 and 4 were re-roofed and the 70-foot turntable in shed 4 was renewed. The complex was closed to steam during June 1967 and the newer shed was used as a diesel depot. After refurbishment, sheds 3 and 4 presently house the main building of the National Railway Museum. In 1998 the remainder of the site, which had closed in 1984, was also acquired by the National Railway Museum. Class A1 4-6-2 locomotive no. 60129 *Guy Mannering* and Class V2 2-6-2 locomotive no. 60828 are depicted in the photograph taken on July 19, 1965 by Bill Wright.

Above and below YORK STATION

In the photograph above, taken on March 6, 1965, Class B1 4-6-0 locomotive no. 61329 is entering the bay platform no 11 at York station. To the right are the through platforms nos 14, 15 and 16. Below, in a view dating from June 3, 1965 Class K1 2-6-0 locomotive no. 62062 is at the end of the former no. 14 platform. The building on the left behind the locomotive is presently part of the National Railway Museum. Both pictures by Geoff Warnes.

BIBLIOGRAPHY

Anderson, Robert and Peter Rose. *Railway Memories No. 22: Return to Leeds.* 2009.

Bairstow, Martin. *The Keighley and Worth Valley Railway: A Guide and History.* 1991.

Bairstow, Martin. *Railways Around Whitby Volume One.* 1998.

Binns, Donald. *The 'Little' North Western Railway: Skipton-Ingleton, Clapham-Lancaster & Morecambe.* 1982.

Bradley, V.J. *Industrial Locomotives of Yorkshire Part A The National Coal Board including Opencast Disposal points & British Coal in West and North Yorkshire.* 2002

Buck, Martin and Mark Rawlinson. *Line by Line: The East Coast Main Line Kings Cross to Edinburgh.* 2002.

Buck, Martin and Mark Rawlinson. *Line by Line: The Midland Route London St. Pancras to Glasgow Central.* 2004.

Dow, George. *Great Central Volume One: The Progenitors 1813-1863.* 1985.

Goode, C.T. *Railways in South Yorkshire.* 1975

Griffiths, Roger and Paul Smith. *The Directory of British Engine Sheds and Principal Locomotive Servicing Points: 2.* 2000.

Haigh, Alan J. *Railways and Tramways in the City of Leeds.* 2010.

Hallas, Christine. *The Wensleydale Railway.* 2002.

Hoole, K. *A Regional History of the Railways of Great Britain Volume 4 The North East.* 1965.

Hoole, Ken. *The Whitby, Redcar and Middlesbrough Union Railway.* 1981.

Industrial Railway Society. *Industrial Locomotives Including preserved and minor railway locomotives.* 2012

Industrial Railway Society. *Industrial Railways and Locomotives of South Yorkshire The Coal Industry – 1947-1964.* 2007.

Joy, David. *A Regional History of the Railways of Great Britain Volume 8 South and West Yorkshire.* 1975.

Mason, P.G. *Lost Railways of East Yorkshire.* 1997.

Platt, John B. *Thorne's First Railway. Thorne and District Local History Association Occasional Papers no. 9.* 1991.

Quick, Michael. *Railway Passenger Stations in Great Britain: A Chronology.* 2009.

Rowley, A. (ed.) *Yorkshire Steam A Nostalgic look at Railways in the Ridings* Vols 1-5. (n.d.).

Smith, Andrew and Roy Etherington, Eds., *Industrial Railway Society Preliminary Draft Industrial Railways and Locomotives of West Yorkshire.* 2004.

Wrottesley, John. *The Great Northern Railway Volume 1 Origins and Development.* 1979.

Also available from Great Northern by Peter Tuffrey

The Last Days of Scottish Steam

Gresley's A3s

visit *www.greatnorthernbooks.co.uk* for details.